The Story of Exeter Speedway
Volume I

The Story of Exeter Speedway
Volume I
The Non-League Years 1929-1945

Tony Lethbridge

ALI-KAT Publications

Ali-Kat Publications
'Tresco'
6 Lower Kings Avenue
Exeter EX4 6JT
England

ISBN 0 9515149 0 3

Photosetting by 'The Works', Exeter, Devon.
Printed and bound by A. Wheaton & Co Ltd., Exeter Devon.

Contents

DEDICATION

This book is for my father, Ted, whose enthusiasm for Exeter Speedway over sixty years is as great today as in 1929. Happily some of it has rubbed off onto me.

ACKNOWLEDGEMENTS

Many people have helped me during the ten years it has taken to get this first volume of the history of Exeter Speedway from dream to reality, and my thanks go to them all. Mr Sidney Salter is probably responsible for the idea in the first place when in 1979 he gave into my safe keeping a magnificent scrapbook and several programmes from the very early days at the County Ground. The late Mr Ron Chanin also provided a great deal of rare material as did Mr Bailey and Mr Tallis. Several pioneer riders have helped. Among them were Freddie Hawken, Gordon Taylor and Richard 'Buggie' Fleeman while sadly others including 'Broncho' Slade, Reg Robins and Jack Addison are no longer around to see the finished work.

My colleagues in the Westcountry Studies Library of Devon Library Services, particularly Ian Maxted, Margaret Westcott, Peter Waite and Tony Rouse, have been infinitely patient and helpful. My thanks also go to those anonymous speedway correspondents of the Express & Echo and the Devon & Exeter Gazette who wrote such detailed and interesting match reports back in pre war days.

My good friend Glyn Shailes has been a wealth of information and encouragement. Glyn generously loaned many of the photographs. Thanks for the loan of photos also go to Julian Thomas and Mrs Diane Parker.

Mike and Karen Bayliss, and the staff of "The Works" have done a splendid job on the technical side of producing this book. Special thanks go to my wife Christine for her patience and proof reading. Last but certainly not least to Ted and Dick Lethbridge who not only remember pre-war speedway but backed my project.

CHAPTER ONE

IN THE BEGINNING

The origins of Exeter Speedway like every other track lay 10,000 miles away in the country town of West Maitland, New South Wales. Although records show that motorcycle races were held on an oval dirt track in Pietermaritzburg, South Africa as early as 1907, and that this kind of racing was popular in the USA around 1909, West Maitland is generally considered to be the birthplace of speedway as we know it.

The whole thing was the brain-child of the incomparable Johnnie S. Hoskins. In 1923 Hoskins, a New Zealander by birth, arrived at Maitland in strange circumstances. Unemployed he had gone to Sydney railway station, laid his last few shillings on the counter and asked the booking clerk for a ticket as far as that would take him. It took him to Maitland where he lost no time in finding himself a job as secretary of the local Agricultural Society.

At that time the Society was heavily in debt to the local bank, and Hoskins immediate task was to put it back on a sound financial footing. One of his fund raising ideas was for Electric Light Carnivals — Saturday night extravaganzas which included athletics, cycle and trotting races under floodlights at the Showground. It did not take long for some local motorcycle owners to suggest the inclusion of bike races as well. These were an immediate success. The competitors rode to the track where they stripped their machines of such unnecessary extras as lights and mudguards before taking to the track. Hopefully they could still be ridden home after the meeting. Within eighteen months the dirt track racing had become so popular that the Society had been able to pay off its debts and also improve the track. A safety fence was installed, the corners banked and the track resurfaced with cinders. This led to Billy Lamont trying out a new method of cornering. Riding his AJS he turned on the power going into the bends and went round in one long controlled slide. 'Broadsiding' had been invented.

The new sport soon became so popular that other tracks were opened. These varied in length from 1/3 of mile to full mile circuits. In 1925 the first purpose built speedway was opened at Newcastle, NSW, with Hoskins as manager. The first meeting attracted 44,000 people.

The big fast tracks were proving so popular that when A. J. Hunting announced that he was opening the first 1/4 mile circuit at the Brisbane Exhibition Grounds many considered that such a small track would lack spectacle. Contrary to expectations the Brisbane venture was a great success attracting regular crowds of 30,000 during the 1926/27 season.

In July 1927 an Englishman, Stanley Glanfield, set out to ride around the world in 120 days on a Rudge-Whitworth combination. Glanfield, a partner in the London motorcycle firm of Glanfield and Lawrence, landed in Australia at Port Darwin and rode the 3,700 miles to Sydney, in all probability the first solo motorcyclist to complete the journey. On arrival in Brisbane he was intrigued by the reports he heard of the local speedway and ventured along to see for himself. Glanfield immediately grasped the potential of the sport and before leaving met with A. J. Hunting and discussed the possibilities of introducing speedway to Britain. The outcome of these discussions was that Hunting and a party of riders, including Frank Arthur, Billy Lamont, and Noel Johnson, sailed for England aboard the S.S. Oronsay arriving in early 1928. Among their fellow passengers were Johnnie Hoskins and Ron Johnson.

Stanley Glanfield himself returned to London in December

1927. He went on to become the promoter of the Coventry (Brandon) Speedway and also set up the first workshop exclusively for the maintenance of speedway machines at his Tottenham Court Road premises.

What is generally regarded as Britain's first speedway meeting took place at High Beech in Epping Forest on Sunday 19 February 1928. Such was the impact of the new sport that over sixty tracks opened that summer including Wimbledon, London White City and Harringay. These three were run by A. J. Hunting who employed Glanfield's brother Leonard as his announcer. Leonard Glanfield had been born in Exeter and knew the city well.

In the autumn of 1928 he decided to open a track of his own and his thoughts returned to the city of his birth. Writing in a 1929 Exeter programme he described his decision thus;

"It had many times occurred to me that this — the County Ground — could be converted into an ideal speedway. The decision to definitely take action came to me, peculiarly enough, one Sunday afternoon at tea and the impulse was so strong that I took the first train to Exeter on Monday morning. This was in November last year. After much preliminary negotiation and argument etc., I obtained a lease from the Exeter Football Club for the use of the County Ground as a Speedway. I then got together some of my friends and immediately formed a Company to handle the proposition."

These friends included Mr F. P. Cottey and Mr Henley who became directors of the company which became known as Southern Speedways Ltd. Glanfield had secured a five year lease at £300 per annum for one meeting a week with an extra £10 to pay for every second meeting it might be decided to hold. Southern Speedways were, under the lease, given the option of renewal at the end of five or ten years on the same terms. These terms were considered extremely favourable to the new venture.

The County Ground Stadium was built in 1898 and in 1929 looked much as it does today, the present grandstand having been completed in 1921 replacing an ornate wooden structure which had been destroyed by fire in 1918. Another smaller stand was on the site of the present greyhound bar.

A tennis court was laid out on what is now the pits area and a vegetable garden, which was later to cause considerable trouble surrounded the first and second bends. Glanfield's interest however centred on the quarter mile asphalt cycling track which ran around the perimeter of the rugby pitch.

Working on ripping up the asphalt and laying the speedway track commenced in late January 1929. The corners were widened from 24 to 40 feet while the width of the straights was increased by five feet to 28 feet. The old surface having been removed a layer of ground cinders was put down and rolled in. On top of this was laid a fine layer of ash and cinders to a depth of two inches. This was slightly deeper on the bends to assist broadsiding. Although the depth of the racing surface was some ten inches. The total lap distance measured 413 yards.

A safety fence was constructed around the completed circuit using stout timber on the corners and heavy mesh on the straights. Forty special floodlights, each of 500 watts, were erected by Frank Buckland of the Southern Electrical Engineering Company. For Buckland, a noted local rugger player, it was the start of a varied career with Exeter Speedway. Finally a Marconiphone public address system was installed and within two months the new set-up was ready for its first meeting.

The new enterprise received enthusiastic support from the press. The Express & Echo of 21 January 1929 reported that:

'Mr Glanfield intends to introduce to Exeter sportsmen at the County Ground all the International speedway stars and exactly the same programme will be served up at Exeter as is provided in London, where the crowds to witness the racing repeatedly exceed 50,000.'

Expectations of that kind of attendance at the County Ground were a shade optimistic but crowds of around 10,000 would be the norm in 1929.

The opening of the new Speedway was set for Saturday

9 March but the sporting public were given the opportunity of a preview a week earlier when two riders took to the track for a short demonstration immediately after a Devon v Gloucester rugby match. The first two riders ever to lap the County Ground were Freddie Hore, an Exonian who had emigrated to Australia became a rider and returned with the first group of Aussie riders, and Bert Spencer, a 16 year old Australian who was nicknamed the 'Baby Cyclone'. Such was the impact of this brief demonstration that word soon got around and when the gates of the stadium opened the following week, hundreds of people were eagerly waiting to see their first speedway meeting.

Indeed the week leading up to the opening night saw a growing awareness of the new sport throughout the surrounding districts. Large advertisements in the local papers proclaimed the 'Cracks' or star riders that would be competing, while other businesses took advantage of the new craze to push their wares. Milletts were selling all the protective gear as supplied to Southern Speedways. On sale were leather jackets at 55/6d (£2.57p) and breeches at 50/- a pair. Approved racing boots complete with steel toe-caps cost 37/6 (£1.87p) a pair while ACU approved crash helmets were 28/6 (£1.42). Jack Gardner meanwhile had the foresight to anticipate big crowds heading towards St Thomas and placed adverts in the papers inviting the public to visit his tailors shop in Fore Street on their way to the meeting.

Prior to the start of racing a dinner was held at the Royal Clarence Hotel after which the Mayor or Exeter, Councillor J. Shirley Steele-Perkins, toasted the success of the speedway and praised the promoters for their determination in bringing it to the city. He pointed out that Devonshire people were "a little bit slow on the uptake and they will look at the thing a little bit critically for some time before they step in and support it. Still it is a novelty and at the beginning the meetings will attract large crowds." He went on to say that anything which amused the populace would have the blessing of the authorities.

Mr Cottey in reply said that there was a need for the sport

in the city as although there were sixty tracks already in operation the nearest were at Bristol and Swindon. He tactfully added that the ACU were very much against betting at speedway meetings and that officials were empowered to remove gamblers from the ground.

Down at the County Ground the paying public started to pass through the turnstiles. Price of admission on the opening night was 2/- and 3/- (10p and 15p) for the Grandstand, or 1/- and 1/6d for the ground. Programmes cost just 2d (1p), and were fairly basic comprising two sheets of paper. The front cover featured an action photo of a rider and an advert for the next meeting. Inside were several advertisements, a list of officials and a outline of the rules as well as more importantly the riders in each of the twenty two races.

The atmosphere in the stadium increased as the crowds poured in. The arrival of the civic party was greeted by loud cheering. The party included the Mayor and Mayoress, the Sheriff (Mr J. T. W. Templeman) and his lady, Sir Robert Newman Bart. M.P. for Exeter, Mr Nicholson the Chief Constable, Sir James and Lady Owen, Mr and Mrs Arthur Brock, the Directors of the Speedway and several other prominent citizens. Shortly before 8.00 pm and in front of over 11,000 eager spectators the Mayoress cut a white silken ribbon to declare the track open and wished the venture every success.

The parade of riders followed and what an impressive line-up it was. From Australia there were Frank Arthur, Ron Johnson, Buzz Hibberd and the Spencer brothers, Bert and Eric. England was represented by Jim Kempster, Roger Frogley, Allan Kilfoyle, Les Dallimore, Tommy Croombs and Les Blakeborough. From South Africa was Les Barker. Several local riders were also on parade. Apart from Freddie Hore they were 'Buggie' Fleeman, Len Clarke, Roy Reeves (Torquay), Harry 'Happy' Kirk (Tiverton), Paul Brockington (Taunton) and E.H.Jones from South Molton.

The evening's entertainment centred around the two main events, the Exeter Handicap and the Golden Helmet Scratch Race. Both were individual competitions comprising four heats, two semi-finals and the final. These were spread out throughout the evening and were interspersed with match races, junior events and lap record attempts; the finals being the climax of the meeting. This would be the pattern for meetings throughout 1929. The main difference between the two major events being that in the handicap races the competitors were pushed off from the start at varying intervals whereas in the scratch events a rolling start was employed where the riders approached the start in line and at the drop of the flag roared away. This was prior to the introduction of the mechanical starting gate and clutch starts were rarely used.

At last the great moment had arrived. Announcer Paddy Parkes introduced the riders for heat one of the Exeter Handicap and then according to one reporter "the fun commenced, became fast and furious, in a very short time the spectators became amused and then enthralled." That first heat was won by Les Dallimore, who started off on a 3 second handicap, from Freddie Hore and his winning time for the four laps was 88.0 seconds. Dallimore went on to win the Final from Ron Johnson.

It is difficult to appreciate today the impact of that first race on the crowd. Very few had probably ever seen a professional motorsport event before and even the floodlighting was a considerable novelty to many of those present. But imagine the thrill it must have been to watch those long framed machines sliding around the big County Ground track throwing up rooster tails of cinders, the riders at full stretch, all of course legtrailing, the roar of the unsilenced engines and the smell of the Castrol R. "Thrilling, breathtaking, hair raising!" was how the Devon and Exeter Gazette described it. The report went on; "These words are not sufficient, and the English language lacks a word that will aptly describe the feeling instilled into spectators of dirt track racing."

The hero of the evening turned out to be Ron Johnson. He obviously impressed the Gazette reporter who wrote; "Johnson gave an exhibition of grit that is typical of the sons of the Empire. It was amazing to watch this dare-devil in his broadsiding. His machine went over at seemingly impossible angles defying all laws of gravity, throwing up the dirt and emitting flames. Having returned to the vertical he would rush up the straight and deliberately throw himself into a dangerous skid. At times his machine was like a recalcitrant horse leaping in the air in a wild endeavour to unseat the rider."

Having lost out to Dallimore in the Handicap Final Johnson made up for it by winning the Golden Helmet in fine style from Eric Spencer. The crowd showed their appreciation when the helmet was placed on his head by the Mayoress.

While Johnson and Dallimore took the major honours, Frank Arthur also made a considerable impression. The 'Wizard' as Arthur was known was one of the classiest riders of the period and it was he who Leonard Glanfield invited to make the first one lap track record attempt. Arthur established a time of 20.6 seconds and also beat Bert Spencer in a special Challenge Match Race.

The meeting was not without incident. There were several spectacular crashes, fortunately without injury to the riders involved. At the end of the evening the crowd left the stadium thrilled by their first taste of speedway racing and eager to return for more. Exeter Speedway had become a reality.

CHAPTER TWO

THE HIGH SUMMER OF 1929

Having got Exeter Speedway off to a flying start Leonard *Wed 13/3*
Glanfield now had to establish the sport in the city on a
regular basis. He planned to stage meetings twice a week
on Wednesdays and Saturdays. Little time was lost in
putting this idea into practice and the second meeting took
place on Wednesday 13 March. The big stars have always
been a draw at the County Ground and Glanfield wasted no
time in bringing 'Wizard' Frank Arthur back to top the bill.
Arthur faired much better on this occasion than on the
opening night. Having thoroughly sorted out his Harley
Davidson 'Peashooter' machine he was unbeaten in both
the Exeter Handicap and the Golden Gauntlets. Arthur also
reduced his own single lap record to 19.8 seconds. Not so
lucky was Torquay's Roy Reeves who was carried off with
back injuries after crashing into the fence during a duel with
Jim Kemspster.

Frank Arthur maintained his impressive form the follow- *Sat 16/3*
ing Saturday when he reduced the one lap record still
further to 19.0 seconds, and again won the principal event,
the Golden Sash. He was billed to take part in a revenge
match with Ron Johnson, winner of the Golden Helmet the
previous week. Alas it was not to be as during the evening
Johnson was badly injured. As he was entering the first
bend his chain snapped and gashed his foot so badly that
he was taken to the Royal Devon and Exeter Hospital

where his little toe was later amputated. This incident caught the imagination of the public and many gruesome tales have been told about it. Even the revered Tom Stenner related one version of the story in his famous book 'Thrilling the million'.

'He (Johnson) always rides in football boots, another peculiarity entirely his own, and after winning a race some time ago dismounted somewhat painfully. His mechanic, full of concern, was about to ask what the trouble was when he caught site of Johnson's right foot.

Half of the boot was missing and most of his sock, and the mechanic went down on his knees to inspect the damage. He had hardly touched the ground when his eyes almost popped out of his head.

"Say, Ron," he shouted, "how many toes have you got?" "Five, of course," was the answer. "One big one, and four little ones, same as you".

Just then Johnson felt a nasty twinge in his right foot, and dropped to his knees too to have one of the biggest shocks of his life. The big toe was there alright and so were three others, but the little one on the end was missing.

After a second's dumbfound amazement, Johnson remembered that he had hit the fence during the race, but in the excitement of the moment had thought no more of it. But here he was without a toe, which was not found until his mechanic had made a careful inspection of the track, and discovered the missing member tucked away under the safety fence.'

Of such are speedway legends made.

There was a short break in racing following this meeting for some minor alterations to the track. Extra boards were added to the safety fence to create a ramp similar to that at the bottom of a 'Wall of Death' thus enabling any rider who ran wide on the bends to use it as an extension of the banking. The improvements were completed in time for the Easter weekend during which two meetings were held, on the Monday as well as the Saturday. Although no 'Frank Arthurs' were appearing the two meetings attracted a total audience of some 19,000 people.

Three new Australians, Hilary 'Whiskey' Buchanan, Harold Stevens and Boyd Pratt appeared at Exeter for the first time but had an unlucky evening as all were involved in minor accidents. Another new attraction was the appearance of sidecar ace Arthur Notorman. Notorman had won a sidecar event at the inaugural High Beech meeting and for his County Ground appearance was programmed to race against G. A. Angel of London. Alas Angel had to withdraw at the last moment due to engine trouble, so instead the extremely popular Coventry rider Lew Lancaster agreed to take on Notorman using his solo machine.

All went well with Notorman taking an early lead on his 498cc Triumph, but in a thrilling finish Lancaster tried to cut between the sidecar and the fence entering the home straight. This manoeuvre did not quite come off and both machines crossed the line locked together. The sidecar passenger was thrown from his perch and slid along the track for some twenty yards, while Notorman struggled to prevent both machines from crashing.

It was not Lancaster's night as his rear wheel spindle broke up and cost him a certain victory in the Silver Star scratch final which was won instead by Fred Ralph.

Lady racers also made their debut at this meeting with Miss Nora Barber from Coventry, the lady champion of the north, defeating her opponent Phyllis Cook.

Glanfield had engaged a nucleus of riders who would prove to be the backbone of Exeter Speedway in 1929. These included the Australians Noel Johnson, Jack Bishop and 'Hard Luck' Harold Stevens, the latter earning his nickname from the number of times he had problems with his machinery. Another Exeter based rider with an unusual nickname was South African Les 'Kernel' Barker. Barker's nickname originated from a current court case which had caused considerable interest involving as it did a woman confidence trickster who dressed as a man and called herself 'Colonel Barker'. Buggie Fleeman, Roy Reeves and Happy Kirk were also regulars but the local rider to make the biggest impact that season was Frank 'Buster' Buckland, the man who had constructed the County Ground floodlights.

17

Buster had been born in Exeter in 1903 and his father had been the caretaker of Rougemont Castle. He proved to be a good rugby player and played regularly at the County Ground before the coming of the speedway. Buckland's involvement with the lighting led him to take an interest in the new sport. In a programme article later in the season he explained his conversion to the cinder sport.

"When the initial practising and racing started at this track I was completely ignorant of exactly what took place having never witnessed a meeting before, and after some little time, I really began to feel that I could do something at it myself. With this idea in mind, I approached Mr Glanfield, who did his best to discourage me. However, with his permission, I borrowed Buggie Fleeman's old A.J.S. and his riding kit and came out on the track in fear and trembling. Before starting off Mr Glanfield, laughing at me, made a bet that I would not go round in under 27 seconds that night. To my surprise I went round on only the second or third lap in 24 seconds. I was then put in the Novice's Scratch Race at the following meeting in which on Dinnis' James I won my heat and came second in the final. I managed to win my next Novice's Scratch Race both heat and final. I was then put in the major part of the programme and am able to say that I have met with some good luck and moderate success."

Wed 24/4   Frank Arthur was back again on Wednesday 24 April. An indication of his popularity was shown by an attendance of nearly 12,000. The Express and Echo reported that the grandstand was packed well before the 7.15pm start time and many patrons were forced to stand. Once again the 'Wizard' was in unbeatable form. He reduced his own one lap record from 19.0 seconds to 18.4. and won both the handicap and the Silver Trophy scratch race. In doing so Arthur beat the Wembley star Colin Watson in the fast time of 76.6. from a flying start. A contemporary reporter described Arthur's broadsiding as 'to say the least sensational'.

Local riders were particularly impressive in this meeting. The performances of Buckland, Len Clarke, Happy Kirk and Eddie Jones were reported as being 'highly praiseworthy'.

Heavy rain kept the dirt down and made for fast times on *Sat 27/4* the following Saturday evening. Buckland was in great form, and after just four meetings he won the handicap final, narrowly beating Bishop to the line in a time of 89 seconds. The meeting was not without incident. Eddie Jones, the South Molton novice fell off in the last lap of the final, and a member of the track staff pulled him up the track to the fence to get him out of the way. Unhappily for Jones, Bishop crossed the line flat out in an attempt to catch Buckland on the run in and continued flat out around the first bend where the Australian promptly ran into the unfortunate Jones who was still prostrate on the cinders and dragged him along the track, It looked serious and although Jones was taken to hospital, he was released the next day suffering only from slight shock and abrasions.

Bishop had earlier won the premier event of the meeting, the Gold Star, beating Buckland in the final to even the honours.

Sidecar racing was also on the programme. A match race took place between Vic Newman with Reg Lovell as his passenger, and Roy Ferguson passengered by Len Wadland. As a safety precaution the outfits started from opposite sides of the track. Newman recorded a time of 99.0 seconds and was declared the winner.

'Cyclone' Billy Lamont, the Australian who had invented *Wed 1/5* broadsiding at West Maitland in the early days, made his County Ground debut on Mayday, but instead of breaking records as intended he merely broke bikes. Altogether Lamont used four machines during the meeting but failed to win any of the finals, although he did manage to win his scratch race heat.

Jack Bishop continued his superb run, winning his third successive premier event. This time he won the Gold Helmet which was presented to him by Sir Edgar Plummer before a vociferous 11,000 strong crowd. Noel Johnson was the winner of the handicap final.

Rain again effected the attendance the next weekend, *Sat 4/5* but even so 7,000 fans assembled to watch the racing. Noel Johnson improved on Wednesday's handicap victory by winning the principle award, the Silver Star. This was Johnson's first major win since coming to England with A.J. Hunting at the beginning of the previous season. Johnson beat the popular Lew Lancaster in the final and received his trophy from 'Jan Stewer', the well known local writer and actor, A. J. Coles.

This meeting was marred by an unfortunate incident in one of the heats. Harold Stevens was riding neck and neck with Torquay's Roy Reeves when the latter fell. Stevens looked set for victory but a steward, on his own authority, put out the red flag causing the race to be stopped. In the rerun Hard Luck Harold was forced out with engine trouble.

It was at this meeting that the famous carthorse novelty race took place. Three track officials were mounted on one horse, and three pushers-off on another while a third was ridden by three dirt track stars. The gun which heralded the start of this unusual event frightened the horses, with the result that two of the officials immediately fell off their mount while the white horse ridden by the pushers-off bolted onto the centre green. The riders' horse actually continued around the track for some distance before taking to the grass and throwing its jockeys. Two of the pushers-off were thrown and one was kicked in the leg, but after treatment was able to walk. The lone official won.

Wed 8/5   Jack Bishop returned to his winning ways at the Wednesday meeting when he won his fourth major prize at the County Ground when some open throttle riding was rewarded with the Gold Gauntlets. Bishop also thrilled the 12,000 crowd with some daring riding in his match races with star attraction 'Broadside' Vic Huxley. In the first heat Bishop took the lead to the delight of the crowd, but after two laps crashed leaving Huxley to finish alone. The second heat was practically a repeat although Huxley led throughout.

Huxley also made an attempt on Frank Arthur's track records, but a fall in the first attempt prevented him making any impact. Falls were common place at this meeting. Reeves crashed badly in the second heat of the Gold Gauntlets scratch race and P. Goodfellow, (who obviously was!) laid his machine down to avoid him.

Harold Stevens had yet another difficult meeting. Stevens' machine developed engine trouble on the last lap of his handicap heat while leading Boyd Pratt. The same thing happened in his scratch race heat. This time the race was won by Freddie Hawken, the well known Newton Abbot all round motor cycle racer, while Stevens pushed his machine around for a lap and a half to be rewarded with second place as he finished within the regulation time of five minutes. Happily it was not a totally unsuccessful evening as Harold went on to beat Buckland in the second semi final of the scratch event.

Frank Arthur returned the next Saturday and faced Jim *Sat 11/5* Kempster in a match race. This proved to be a rare tussle between the two 'cracks'. Arthur won both races by a matter of feet, roaring around the outside as Kempster held tight to the white line. Arthur's victory was all the more creditable as earlier he had been knocked unconscious while attempting to break his own track record. Kempster had tried first but was unable to lower the 'Wizards' time. When Arthur went out he hit a bump on the first lap and crashed into the safety fence. The machine and rider somersaulted and on landing Arthur was dragged along for some distance. The fall knocked him out but he was otherwise unhurt. However his famous Harley Davidson Peashooter was badly damaged and Arthur had to use borrowed machinery for his later races.

The final of the Silver Helmet scratch race turned out to be a frantic affair. This race had an all Australian line-up with Bishop, Arthur, Stevens and Noel Johnson coming to the start. Stevens soon dropped out, but a struggle developed between Bishop and Arthur while Johnson followed close behind. On the last bend of the last lap Bishop hit the fence in a big way. His machine was thrown high into the air and as it came down it hit two spectators who were leaning over the fence. Arthur and Johnson also became involved and crashed. Bishop was stretchered off, but was found to be unhurt. Unfortunately one of the spectators, Daisy Connett, of Feniton, was taken to the

R.D.& E. suffering from concussion, while the other fan, an unnamed man, had a cut face but was not detained. In the rerun Arthur was the clear winner as both Stevens and Johnson had engine trouble. Miss Connett it was reported later was fit enough to answer questions the following day.

Wed 15/5   Kempster returned four days later in place of Colin Watson, who had dislocated his ankle at Wimbledon on the previous Monday. Smiling Jim won the Exeter handicap final but it was Billy Lamont who stole the show by winning the Gold Sash final. He also broke Arthur's four lap flying record. The new time was 7.6 seconds, a fifth of a second under the Wizard's record. This would appear to be quite a fast time for sixty years ago, but it must be remembered that Lamont would have been travelling flat out when he crossed the start line rather than having to build up his speed from a standing start.

Bishop gave Lamont a run for his money in the final, but the Cyclone rounded off a good evening by beating Stevens in a match race.

Sat 18/5   The Whitsun weekend proved to be a busy time for speedway fans as Leonard Glanfield had arranged no less then three meetings in five days. The action got underway on the Saturday evening, with local riders well to the fore. Both Jack Bishop and Jim Kempster were prevented from reaching the final of the Silver Star, although Bishop came out on top when they met in a match race. Noel Johnson achieved his second major win, even though he rode the final without a steering damper. 'Kernel' Barker won the handicap event. It was not a good night for Harold Stevens as he crashed several times.

The General Election campaign was in full swing at this time and Glanfield used its topicality to the full. On this occasion he arranged a 'parliamentary' scratch race between 'Stanley Baldwin', 'Lloyd George' and 'Ramsay MacDonald', the 'leaders' of the Conservative, Labour and Liberal parties. The riders, who wore black masks, were mounted on ordinary dirt track bikes, and the special conditions were that the winner was the last man past the post, that no rider should stop, and that catching hold of the safety fence was prohibited. None of the riders were successful in completing a lap and 'Mr Stanley Baldwin' being the last man to stop, was declared the winner.

Whit Monday saw another good meeting which included appearances by Sig Schlan and Lionel Van Praag. With Exeter now completely in the grip of election fever Glanfield again took advantage of the situation by inviting the retiring MP Sir Robert Newman and the prospective Conservative candidate Mr G. D. Roberts as guests of honour. Impartiality was maintained when both the Liberal and Labour candidates visited other meetings.

A new event on the programme was the Plummer Cup, presented by Sir Edgar and Lady Plummer of Crossmead who were both prominent supporters of the speedway. Their trophy, which was to be competed for on a regular basis by local riders, was won on this occasion by Tiverton's Happy Kirk. Frank Arthur had an off night returning three times with broken chains, while Harold Stevens inevitably attracted all the bad luck that was going. He even missed out on the novelty event! Glanfield being a great showman always tried to put on an interval attraction to amuse the crowd. On this occasion it was claimed that Harold was the reigning Australian bronco busting champion and was down to give a demonstration of his art. Regrettably this event had to be cancelled at the last moment as the management were unable to obtain a wild enough animal. A great variety of novelty events were held during the year ranging from a hoop race for children and a pram race for mothers to that infamous carthorse race. A regular feature which proved tremendously popular with the crowd was an Ariel fitted with eccentric wheels on which the riders took turns each week to set a track record.

In more recent years lady riders have been looked upon as something of a novelty, but in 1929 there were almost regular events with the ladies often racing against the men. The first local ladies race at the County Ground was contested by Miss Manley of Honiton and Miss Phyllis Cook of Bideford. They passed and repassed each other several times during the race but on the last bend, Miss Cook, who was riding a Coventry Eagle, had the misfortune to clip her opponent's back wheel and took a tumble. She pluckily remounted and finished the race to the appreciative applause of the crowd. Miss Manley's winning time for the four laps was 2 minutes 4.4 seconds. The redoubtable Miss Cook defended the honour of the West Country on another occasion against the Lady Champion of the North, Nora Baker of Coventry, but was easily beaten.

Wed 22/5   Speculation had been rife over the previous week for Glanfield had promised that an ace of the calibre of Frank Arthur would appear at the County Ground on Wednesday 22 May. The publicity was not without foundation and 12,000 people arrived to see the Exeter debut of the legendary American Lloyd 'Sprouts' Elder, who along with Arthur was the earliest speedway superstar. The thrill of witnessing 6' 6" Sprouts broadsiding with his knee touching the cinders proved extremely popular, especially as he won both Gold Helmet and the Exeter Handicap finals as well as beating Tiger Sanderson in two straight match races. Elder did however fail to better the track record. In the Gold Helmet final Bishop chased him hard, despite riding the last two laps with a flat tyre. The little Australian had however had his moment of glory earlier in the contest, when in the first semi final he streaked away from Elder at the start. Although the American did his utmost to overtake on the bends Bishop was equal to his every move, and flashed across the finish line several lengths ahead much to the delight of the crowd.

Stevens had bought a new Douglas machine but although he managed to battle through to the final his only reward was a fall.

Elder was presented with his trophy by Mr H. Lloyd Jones, the Labour candidate. Two casualties in the handicap were Boyd Pratt who was taken to hospital with shock and abdominal injuries, after getting into a speed wobble and crashing, while Buggie Fleeman damaged his ankle.

Sat 25/5   Harold Stevens came good the following Saturday when he qualified for both finals and a match race with Bishop, but once again his infamous bad luck struck. In the Gold

Gauntlet final Stevens led for three and a half laps with a flat back tyre, but just yards from the finish the tyre came off the rim and jammed the back wheel, bringing the machine to a halt and allowing Bishop to nip through to win. In the match races which followed the honours were even with one win each, but in the decider Bishop suffered intermittent engine trouble and Stevens was well ahead when 100 yards from the finish his machine stopped and Bishop again went through to win. Afterwards Bishop sportingly called for the race to be rerun on another occasion.

The final of the Exeter Handicap was equally disastrous. Noel Johnson came off and Bishop piled into him, while Stevens laid down his machine to avoid them. Johnson was badly winded but was able to continue. Bishop, however, hurt his shoulder and withdrew. In the rerun Kernel Barker fell and Stevens again threw himself off to prevent a crash. At the third attempt justice prevailed and Hark Luck Harold achieved a popular victory.

The second series of races for the Plummer Cup also took place. Charlie Swift beat Roy Reeves for the right to challenge Happy Kirk, the holder. This race was not concluded as Swift came off after a speed wobble and Kirk skidded onto the grass.

Wednesday was the eve of Election Day but also a most important date in the history of Exeter Speedway, for that evening team racing took place at the County Ground for the first time. The Exeter City Speedway team comprising Barker, Buckland, Fleeman and Swift had drawn 17-17 at Bristol's Knowle Park the previous evening and local supporters were hopeful of seeing Exeter's first victory. They were not to be disappointed The 'inter-city' match was raced over two heats and a final interspersed among the other events on the programme with points scored on a 4-3-2-1 basis. Swift and Barker led Dallimore and Webb home in the opening heat and although Buckland defeated Ted Bravery and S.F. Smith in heat 2 Buggie Fleeman fell off. In the final Barker headed Bravery while Buckland finished third ahead of Webb to give Exeter victory by 17-12.

Wed 29/5

25

Two surprise visitors at this meeting were Jack Parker, one of the England all time greats, and Freddie Hore. Neither had the best of fortune and did not make it to any of the finals. Although it is not recorded in any of the match reports it is possible that an incident occurred during this meeting which Stenner later described in 'Thrilling the Million.'

Parker, who made very few riding appearances at the County Ground was renowned as a practical joker. He fell in the course of one race, but came to no harm and wheeled his bike onto the centre green. Parker had been in front and his fall left the second man with the race in his pocket, but on the third lap he too fell almost at the same spot. The un-named rider jumped up and tried to restart his machine but found that the chain was broken. The two remaining riders were both raw novices and as they passed by in the slow but stately progress the imp of mischief in Parker came to the fore. He offered the other rider his bike. It was gleefully accepted and with a friendly· push from Jack he regained the track and set off in pursuit, to such effect that he regained the lead and won. To the amazement of them both, so the story goes, the switch over went unnoticed by the officials, and a rider that had finished on a machine different to that on which he had started was awarded the race. Later everything was put right and the prize money was handed over to the rightful winner.

Sat 1/6   June heralded a change of fortune for Harold Stevens. He lined up against Buckland, Bishop and Jack Chapman, the holder of the World Mile record, in the Gold Star final, Bishop made the start and led until the second lap, when Stevens having cast caution to the wind rode like a wild man and went to the front where he held off all Bishop's challenges. It was Harold's first since coming to race in England and he was presented with his prize by Mr A. F. Nicholson, the chief constable. Stevens received a rapturous ovation from the crowd on his lap of honour.

Two new faces provided the main attraction. Chapman, the champion of Australia, had set his world mile record on a third of a mile track with a time of 61.4 seconds raced against the former record holder Frank Duckett in a match race series. Chapman led the first heat but Duckett overtook him until Chapman regained the lead on the final lap. Duckett injured his thumb badly between races but still managed to get out in front in the second heat until his engine expired.

Charlie Swift, Buster Buckland, Buggie Fleeman, and Ron Stokes were the finalists in the handicap event, with Swift winning from Stokes after a close fought contest.

The return of the Stevens/Bishop match race turned out to be something of a disappointment as both riders suffered engine problems. However Bishop managed to cross the line first.

A sodden track did not deter a galaxy of stars from putting on some superb riding for the benefit of the 9,000 fans who defied the weather on Wednesday. Billy Lamont and Stan Spencer (Harringay) rejoined Bishop and Stevens to contest the Gold Sash final. This turned out to be a reversal of roles for the popular Exeter pair. After a false start the quartet flashed away with Bishop in front closely followed by Stevens. Lamont came to grief as he tried to get on terms with the leaders. Bishop's lead seemed secure until his chain broke in the last few yards and Stevens nipped through for his second premier victory. *Wed 5/6*

The handicap final brought Lamont, Stevens and Bishop together again along with Roy Reeves. Lamont was off scratch, while Stevens and Bishop had a two second start and Reeves four. Bishop had trouble at the start and retired on the first lap. Reeves and Stevens got away smartly, but Lamont, determined to collect the £10 prize money, stormed between them on the back straight and streaked away to win. The Cyclone went on to beat Frank Duckett in two straight legs of the match race.

Another team match also took place. This time the opposition was an International Speedways Ltd. Select side from Harringay. The I.S.L. team included Bill Burger, Reg Porter, Stan Spencer and Freddie Hore. Exeter won 13-8.

Extensive work on the track produced some unusually fast times with Bishop, Stevens and guest star Colin Watson *Sat 8/6* setting the pace. Bishop, who had just taken delivery of a new Douglas, beat the Harley Davidson mounted Watson in two straight legs of the match race but developed engine problems in the Gold Helmet final. This allowed Stevens to take this third consecutive victory, which he celebrated by completing the double. To do this he beat Ron Stokes in the final of the Exeter handicap. Harold received his prizes from Mr Miles Mander, the celebrated English film star and writer. Such was Bishop's misfortune in recent meetings that it was suggested that he take over the 'Hard Luck' sobriquet.

Wed 12/6   Continuing bad weather had its effect on the next meeting. The track was practically underwater and both Colin Watson and Jack Bishop failed to get their machines going for their heats of the handicap event which was won by Noel Johnson. Bishop sorted his machinery out in time to clean up in the Gold Gauntlet final.

The Exeter team recorded their second win over Bristol, this time by a walk-over 11-3.

Sat 15/6   Noel Johnson won both the Silver Helmet and Handicap finals at that week's Saturday meeting to earn his promotion to 'star' status. Riding his Bitzer machine, built with parts from other motorcycles, he beat both Bishop and Stevens to break their strangle hold on the major events as well as Broadside Vic Huxley. In the handicap he finished alone after Happy Kirk fell and Huxley and Ron Stokes ran into engine problems. Stokes, formerly of Coventry, had started to make his mark at Exeter as had the Taunton novice Reg Beer. Engine problems spoilt the match races between Huxley and Stevens. In the first heat Huxley leapt away from the start, but in the second and the decider motor problems ensured that Stevens had two easy wins.

Sat 22/6   Noel Johnson collected his third big win the following Saturday with victory over Bishop in the Gold Star scratch final. Since his elevation to star status Johnson had been riding exceptionally well, and the final produced a thrilling tussle. The four riders facing the starter were Johnson, Bishop, Jack Addison and the Bristol rider Bill Clibbett. The early pace was extremely hot and as he attempted to keep up Addison slid completely around and landed neatly on the grass. It was a strangely contrasting pair which fought for the lead. Bishop led on his finely tuned Douglas, which emitted a tremendous roar, from Johnson who's Bitzer only gave out a popping sound but seemed to flit over the ground. Jack sat practically upright and threw up masses of dirt at each corner, whereas Noel crouched over his machine, dragging his foot behind him but not broadsiding to any great extent. They raced neck and neck for two laps until Johnson inched ahead and nothing that Bishop attempted could reduce that small lead. It was therefore fitting that Bishop's wife should pin the Gold Star to Johnson's helmet.

A three cornered match race between Stevens, Bishop and Johnson had been planned to decide the track championship. but this did not materialize as Hard Luck Harold crashed into Bert Spencer in an earlier race and smashed up his engine. Instead Bishop beat Johnson in two straight runs.

Buster Buckland retained the Plummer Cup. To do so he beat Charlie Swift who had previously defeated Happy Kirk to qualify.

Jack Addison was another local who was making considerable progress. He had only ridden the County Ground a few times but on this occasion reached both the main finals. In the Exeter handicap he finished second to Ted Bravery who along with his Knowle Park team-mates Bull Clibbett and Jim Douglas had become frequent visitors to Exeter.

Tuesday 25 June saw the staging of the first great *Tues 25/6* Speedway Revel, which turned out to be the high spot of the 1929 season. It was also probably the best supported meeting in the entire sixty year history of Exeter Speedway.

The Revels, of which there were to be four that season, were all action gala evenings involving many of the top riders of the day. Huge advertisements in the press told of the stars that would be appearing, and with the tremendous enthusiasm for speedway which was rife in Exeter at that time it was not surprising that a huge crowd turned up. The queues started forming outside the stadium at 4.00pm and the crowd increased enormously within the next hour. Thirty policemen from the City force were on hand, but the would-be spectators overwhelmed them long before the start time, and a quarter of an hour before the first race the turnstiles had to be closed, as the ground was packed to capacity. From then on only ticket holders were admitted and it was estimated that some three thousand fans had to be turned away. Inside the County Ground between 15000 and 16000 people filled every vantage point. Many in the grandstands were unable to find seats and even the Press found that their seats had been usurped.

The track was in superb condition and there were three main events on the programme, the Gazette Gold Casket Handicap, the Express & Echo Gold Cup Scratch Race and the Pike Victory Column.

The Express & Echo Gold Cup produced a thrilling final. The finalists were Frank Arthur, Eric Spencer, Bishop and Stevens, and all were at the top of their form. Bishop got away at the start with Arthur and Stevens in pursuit. The pace was terrific and the strain on the motors soon started to show. After two laps Jack's machine cracked and from then on only fired on one cylinder. The Wizard took over the lead and Stevens chased him hard until he fell off while overdoing a broadside. Arthur finished well in front, with the full throated roar of his Harley Peashooter reverberating around the stadium. Eric Spencer just slipped passed Bishop at the post. The Echo headlined Arthur's success in their match report as ' "Wizard's" Wizardry '.

The Pike Silver Column for the fastest lap by a Southern Speedways contracted rider was won by Ron Stokes with a time of 20.4 seconds. This trophy had an interesting history. It was donated by Pikes Garage in Alphington Street where many of the riders worked on their bikes. The trophy reappeared in 1982 when a relative of Stokes asked for it to be presented to Andy Campbell to mark his achievement in becoming the Falcons second all time highest scorer in a season. It was handed to Andy by Ivan Mauger, arguably the greatest speedway rider ever.

Buggie Fleeman was the popular winner of the Gazette Gold Casket handicap final, leading all the way from Arthur and Charlie Swift, Bishop having pulled out early with machine failure.

A Silver cup donated by the Dartmouth Naval College for the fastest four laps of the evening was won by Jack Bishop, who tied with Arthur on 81.4 seconds. Jack received the trophy after the Wizard had sportingly decided that they should toss for it. Harold Stevens rounded off a splendid evening with a remarkable ride on the eccentric Ariel.

Immediately after the racing finished a large part of the huge crowd moved on to the famous Dellers Cafe in Bedford Street, where the mayor presented the trophies at the Revel Dance. It was announced that the interval collection taken in aid of the Mayor's Poor Box appeal raised £30 which was increased when Frank Arthur generously donated his prize money from the handicap final.

Dancing took place to the music of a band called the Original Speedway Revellers who played in full 'cinder track kit' of boots, leathers and crash helmets until the heat forced them to divest themselves.

This meeting marked the zenith of Leonard Glanfield's operation at the County Ground.

Some of the Shining Lights
at the
Exeter Speedway.

W. Shillings '29.

F. R. PARKES
(ANNOUNCER)

JACK
BISHOP.

MR LEN
GLANFIELD.
(MANAGING DIRECTOR
SOUTHERN SPEEDWAYS
LTD.)

"WIZARD"
FRANK
ARTHUR.

"BUSTER"
BUCKLAND

NOEL
JOHNSON

HAROLD
STEVENS.

CHAPTER THREE

THE EARLY AUTUMN OF 1929

Normality returned the following Saturday when Glanfield *Sat 29/6* programmed Noel Johnson and Colin Watson together in a match race series. Watson, who was described as a pupil of Wizard Frank Arthur and rode a similar Harley Davidson Peashooter, was beaten in two straight races, but he did not have the best of luck. In the first race he shed a tyre when going well and in the second his Harley started to run rough.

However Watson had more success in the Gold helmet where he progressed to the final and faced Stevens, Bishop and Johnson again. Bishop true to form took the lead from the off, but Stevens soon scorched past, with Watson third. Starting the third lap Bishop overdid it and came down. Harold continued to blast around and finished in the creditable time of 83 seconds. Watson meanwhile lost second place to Johnson when the Harley again started to give trouble.

The Handicap final was fought out between Johnson, Bishop, Ron Stokes and Ken Purser, a Southampton rider who had earlier caused a stir when having been given a six second start in his heat, had walked away with the race. The final was a different matter. Purser could do no better than third. Stokes won from Bishop, the latter having found the Coventry rider's four second start just too much to make up, while Johnson fell off.

Other casualties of the evening were Freddie Hore, making a welcome reappearance at his home town track, and Jack Addison who tumbled and had the misfortune to be ridden into by Watson.

Buggie Fleeman and local junior Allan Collier caused great excitement with their attempts on the one lap record using the 'buck jumping' Ariel. Fleeman achieved a time of 54 seconds and Collier 55.4., both well outside Bingley's record of 35.0

Harold Stevens was presented with his Gold Helmet by the Rev. T. Cawley, the curate at nearby St Thomas church. The reverend gentleman, who was a regular speedway fan, announced over the microphone that on the coming Sunday a service of thanksgiving for the remarkable recovery of King George V from septicaemia, would be held at the stadium. Mr Cawley went on to thank Mr Glanfield for allowing the organisers the free use of the public address system. The speedway promoter had also generously undertaken to meet the cost of printing the hymn sheets so that the whole of the collection could go to the hospital's funds.

Wed 3/7 Stevens became the first rider to achieve the distinction of notching his second double when he won both the Silver Trophy and Exeter Handicap finals. Harold was comfortably leading the scratch final when the rest of the field fell and the race had to be rerun. Again the big Australian made the start, this time with Ron Stokes in hot pursuit. Ron made an all out bid to take the lead but fell in the attempt.

Stoke was at this time making a considerable impact on the local fans. Earlier he had ridden a wonderful race against Frank Arthur and had the satisfaction of recording the fastest time of the meeting, 88.8 seconds.

Harold Stevens took advantage of Arthur's over handicaping and stormed away from Bill Clibbett and Southampton's Ken Purser in the final.

Heavy rain fell just before start time rendering the track incapable of fast times. Despite the weather between 7,000 and 8,000 people braved the elements to watch the main attraction, a match race between Frank Arthur and fellow

Aussie Max Grosskreutz who was making his first appearance at the Exeter track. As joint holders of the world mile record on quarter mile tracks it had been planned that they should make a new attempt, but this was ruled out by the conditions. That apart the Australian pair put on a dazzling display in their match race series. Arthur narrowly won the first leg but suffered engine problems in the second. Grosskreutz led the decider but although he did not look very much at home on the banking, held the Wizard off in thrilling style to win.

Although Max failed to make it to either of the finals, it was noted that his style of riding clearly marked him out as a 'star'.

Fay Taylour, who was recognised as the best lady rider in the world made her Exeter debut on Saturday 6 July. Unfortunately Fay was unable to show her true form as while practicing earlier in the afternoon her machine had given trouble. Happily the situation was remedied by Miss Hull, an aspiring local rider, who made her similar Douglas available. *Sat 6/7*

Prior to the meeting Miss Taylour was allowed a few laps to accustom herself with the different machine and soon proved that she knew how to ride.

Fay had been programmed to ride a match race series against popular Buggie Fleeman, who won the first leg fairly easily. The second proved more interesting by reason of the number of incidents. This race was rerun no less than four times when Miss Taylour had engine trouble then took a couple of falls while in the lead. One of these crashes took place directly in front of Fleeman who gallantly and 'with a great effort threw himself from his machine to avoid running over the fallen lady'. The crowd were not slow to show their approval, and Fay shook him by the hand. At the last attempt Fay went all out from the start, setting such a pace that Buggie could not close the gap. In the decider Fay again streaked away but on the third lap Buggie overtook her. Alas as he reached the finish line his front tyre burst. He went into an uncontrolable wobble, and came down heavily after being thrown over the handlebars. Fleeman was carried from the track but fortunately had only been winded.

Jack Bishop won the Gold Gauntlet final in masterly fashion from Noel Johnson, Frank Buckland and Lew Lancaster. It was noted that Alf Chick, the Wembley star, did not shine as expected.

Wed 10/7   In perfect weather Frank Buckland's brilliant riding was the highlight of the mid-week meeting. Not everything however was perfect. A sudden heat wave left the track dry and hard and the crowd was down to between 4,000 and 5,000.

Buckland started off by beating Ron Stokes in two straight legs of their match race. In fairness to Stokes, it was pointed out that the Coventry man took a heavy fall in an intervening heat and twisted his leg, but rather than disappoint the fans insisted on riding the second leg.

Buckland easily won the handicap final and then made Harold Stevens work very hard for his victory in the Silver Helmet final. Bishop was again out of luck with yet another snapped chain costing him a place in the final. Ken Purser again impressed while Tom Fardon, later to become one of England's greatest riders, made a welcome appearance but fell while leading his semi-final of the Exeter Handicap. Swift and Lancaster were also involved in a spectacular pile-up but neither was injured. With Mr Glanfield on the continent in search of new talent, the duties of clerk of the course were taken over by Mr D. C. Lorkin, the secretary of Southern Speedways. It was announced that Len Clarke, who was injured in a crash several weeks before, had been released from the R.D.& E. Hospital and had gone to a convalescent home in Torquay. He had been conveyed there by car thanks to the kindness of the Exeter Rotary Club.

Sat 20/7   The dry spell had caused several problems with the track and it was decided to cancel the weekend meeting so that the racing strip could be sorted out.

Wed 24/7   Wednesday 24 July saw Leonard Glanfield introduce a new type of event, an international contest between England and Australia for 'the Ashes'. It was not a test match in the modern sense, but a series of match races between riders from the countries concerned. The 'Ashes' Trophy was won by Jack Bishop after he had beaten fellow

Aussie Harold Stevens in the final. The trophy was presented by the injured Len Clarke who was introduced by the announcer as "one of speedway's most distinguished cripples". Despite this accolade Clarke received a warm reception from the crowd.

The Ashes were run over four heats, semi-finals and finals. The first heat produced a fine tear-up between Frank Buckland representing England and Bishop, with the latter proving just too good for the local man. Noel Johnson beat Jim Kempster convincingly in the second, while Colin Watson, mounted for once on a Douglas, rather than his more familiar Harley, failed to catch Harold Stevens in the third. England's sole success came in heat 4 when Ron Stokes covered himself with glory by streaking away from Whiskey Buchanan, who soon afterwards pulled out with a broken gearbox. Stokes rode on alone but with a lap still to go his gearbox also gave trouble, and he was forced to push his machine the final quarter of a mile to finish in a time of 3 minutes and 3 seconds. His efforts earned scant reward in the semi-final where he fell when a long way behind Stevens. Previously Bishop had seen off Johnson in the first semi, so when the two finalists wheeled their machines to the start the spectators "began to sit up and brace themselves for a big strain on their nerves".

As the riders came round on the rolling lap the air was tense with excitement. Both men shot away from the start and went flat out into the bend where Bishop gained the advantage. But after a couple of laps Stevens made his bid. However he entered a bend far too fast to stay on and thus Bishop finished alone, albeit with a collapsed back wheel. Stevens was the first to offer his congratulations.

Bishop's success continued with a convincing win over Johnson, Happy Kirk and Fred Hawken in the handicap final. The 'B' Grade scratch race was won by Paul Brockington who crashed later in the evening and was stretchered off stunned by a blow to the head.

An unsavoury aspect of this meeting was the 'barracking' which twice broke out from a certain section of the crowd who apparently disagreed with the judges decision.

The second Great Revel Night took place on Tuesday 30 July. This was another star studded occasion, but the man who won the heart of the bumper 11,000 strong crowd was the local favourite, Jack Bishop.

The race which had the fans talking for weeks afterwards was the final of the Chevrolet Gold Cup scratch event. Bishop's chief opponent was no lesser rider than Cyclone Billy Lamont. Lamont made a superb start but Bishop was just inches behind him as they roared on to the back straight. Bishop applied so much pressure that in an effort to shake off his pursuer the Cyclone took a bend much too fast and slid to earth, but was quickly on his feet. While white-coated officials removed Lamont's AJS machine from the track Bishop carried on to win in the remarkably quick time of 83.8 seconds. He was loudly cheered as he rode round to the start-line to collect his trophy from Sir Robert Newman, later Lord Mamhead.

Lamont had meanwhile returned to the pits, but as Bishop sat astride his machine waiting for the presentation there was a pause. It was seen that the telephone link to the pits was in use. The crowd anticipated the announcer and shouts of 'Jack is offering Billy a rerun' echoed around the ground. The assumption was correct and Lamont crossed the centre green where he spoke to Leonard Glanfield before taking the microphone. He told the crowd "Jack Bishop, sportsman as he is, has offered me a rerun. Jack has won fair and square therefore I cannot accept his offer." It was a sporting gesture on the part of Bishop, while Lamont it was noted acted with equal sportsmanship by turning it down.

In the heats leading up to the final Bishop had out manoeuvred and out paced Stamford Bridge 'crack' Gus Kuhn. Roger Frogley and Harold Stevens had met in the first heat and a bad start had given the Exeter man a yard and a half advantage which he made the most of. Both Max Grosskreutz and Lamont crashed in their heat but Billy won the rerun. The fourth heat looked like being a duel between Eric Spencer and Noel Johnson, but Spencer fell on the first lap and although he remounted quickly was unable to make up the lost ground.

The first semi-final saw Bishop win easily after Stevens fell early on, while another bad start cost Johnson the second semi. He was left several yards behind which gave Lamont a tremendous advantage.

Bert Spencer led the Handicap final from Swift, Bishop and Purser. After two laps Bishop moved up to second, but a broken chain ruined his chances. Swift too missed out when his tyre came off his back wheel.

The one disappointment of this meeting was the non appearance of American Art Pechar. A stop press announcement in the programme informed patrons that he was still unfit following a crash during a recent match race with Lamont.

The bumper crowds which the speedway was regularly attracting meant that some alterations had to be made to the stadium. Glanfield placed advertisements in the press inviting haulage contractors to dump rubble at the County Ground thus enabling him to build up the back straight terracing. The second Revel also saw the opening of the new Ferndale Road entrance which eased access to the 1/6d popular enclosure.

Mon 5/8

The meeting planned for August Bank Holiday Monday evening was expected to attract a big crowd especially with Cyclone Billy Lamont topping the bill plus the exciting prospect of a team match against Surrey. Unfortunately the holiday weekend weather was very wet and the meeting was abruptly terminated before it was half way through. While the Silver Star scratch race reached the semi final stage only the heats of the Exeter Handicap were run. Jack Bishop beat Lamont in the first heat of their match race, and Alf Metcalfe won the opening heat of the match for Surrey followed home by the Exeter pair of Purser and Buckland.

It was later announced that in future meetings would only be staged once a week on Tuesdays commencing on 13 August.

Sat 10/8

Before this however the Exeter City speedway team achieved a remarkable result when they travelled to Stamford Bridge in London for a match with what was at the time the most successful team in the country. This home and away challenge came about as a result of a £50 wager between Leonard Glanfield and Billy Wells, the Bridge manager. Until Exeter's visit the Stamford Bridge team was unbeaten on their own narrow track around the Chelsea football pitch and had won 12 out of their 13 matches ridden so far in the Southern League, their only defeat having come away at Southampton. The Pensioners were to win all their remaining fixtures and become speedway's first ever league champions.

The evening of Saturday 10 August was a momentous occasion for the Exeter team as they prepared to face the might of the Londoners in front of a 25,000 strong crowd. Exeter, in their red and white colours, were represented by Noel Johnson (captain), Harold Stevens, Bert Spencer and Jack Bishop with Buster Buckland as reserve.

At the drop of the flag in heat 1 Johnson and Spencer grabbed the lead and looked like holding it until Spencer dropped back with engine trouble and was eventually over-taken. Exeter however held the advantage as scoring was on a 4-2-1 principle.

Stevens and Bishop came out next against Gus Kuhn and Colin Ford. Again the Exeter pair went out in front taking full advantage of the narrow track to keep the opposition at bay. Unfortunately over enthusiasm caused them to collide and Stevens lost his footrest. Kuhn saw the change and nipped through for second place, but Harold managed to retain third and extend Exeter's lead.

With the scores at Exeter 9 Stamford Bridge 5 the riders came out for the final. Bishop and Johnson went to the front. Jack led with Noel covering him and holding off the home riders. On the last lap Bert Bolt made an all out attempt to get by, but in an effort to keep him out Johnson came off. Despite this Exeter retained their lead to win 13-8.

Such was their riders achievement that the directors of Southern Speedways held an informal dinner in their honour at the Rougemont Hotel where toasts were drunk and speeches made. Glanfield presented each of his riders with a framed team photograph and predicted that Exeter

40

Speedway would become the best in the world.

Within a few days the Exeter team were again success- *Tues 13/8* ful. This time they beat Cardiff 12-9 at the County Ground. It looked at first as if the Exeter boys were in for an easy time and after two heats were 10-4 up, but in the final heat Nobby Key beat Buster Buckland, and Champ Upham took an unexpected third place when Stevens fell while challenging Key. Jimmy Hindle and George Gregor made up the rest of the Welsh side.

On the individual front Jack Bishop won the Gold Helmet for the second time that year, while Charlie Swift was victorious in the handicap. Key pushed his machine home for second place when it let him down in the last 200 yards and fell down exhausted having just managed to beat Max Grosskreutz who had engine trouble earlier but restarted. Grosskreutz had also made an unsuccessful attempt on the track record.

Exeter collected their second win over Stamford Bridge *Tues 20/8* when they defeated the Londoners 15-6 at the County Ground. Exeter again started well and looked to be heading for maximum points in heat 1 when Bishop and Buckland headed Gus Kuhn and Wal Phillips, but after just half a lap Buckland's machine faltered and he lost ground. Although he got it going again both 'Bridge riders had passed him. Bishop however retained his lead and won in a time of 85 seconds.

Heat 2 produced a real thriller. Stevens and Colin Ford shot away and engaged in a hard fought duel. Stevens led for the first lap, but then Ford going flat out overtook him. Ford's lead was short lived. Hard Luck Harold, thanks to some sensational riding, went back in front and held on to win. Noel Johnson was third ahead of Les Blakeborough.

There was keen excitement as the four riders came round to start the final heat. Bishop and Stevens lined up for Exeter against Kuhn and Ford. Bishop made his customary lightning start and with Stevens tucked in behind left the opposition trailing. This clinched the match for Exeter and the £50 for Leonard Glanfield. Kuhn was third and Ford last after his machine had let him down.

The individual events also produced their fair share of thrills. Charlie Swift was involved in a thrilling dice with Kuhn in which the Exeter man stalked his opponent all the way before roaring around him on the last bend. Bishop rounded off a fine evening by defeating Bert Spencer in the final of the Exeter Trophy, while Buckland qualified in style by beating Welsh champion, Ivor Creek. The handicap final, in which all five contestants started off the scratch mark, also ended in spectacular fashion with Swift dead heating with newly arrived Australian Cyril Anderson.

Sat   24/8

The Exeter City team followed up their success against Stamford Bridge with another away victory the following Saturday when they visited the new Bannister Court track at Southampton. It proved to be an eventful evening.

Bishop and Stevens got Exeter off to another good start by taking maximum points from the opening heat. However Johnson could do no better than third in heat 2, while the Exeter reserve Happy Kirk fell during the last lap. Kirk was replacing Buckland who had crashed early in the meeting and was unable to take his place in the team match. Bishop and Stevens looked set to repeat their heat 1 maximum in the final but Stevens fell and was ridden over by Southampton's Colin Stewart. As a result the popular Australian was taken to hospital with three broken ribs and internal injuries. In the rerun Bishop won enabling Exeter to gain a narrow 10-8 victory. This was Southampton's first defeat on their own track.

During the evening Bishop and Johnson took second and third respectively in the scratch race final. Earlier that afternoon Bishop had ridden at Portsmouth where he had won the main event.

Tues 27/8

Back at the County Ground the following Tuesday the team scored another notable victory. This time it was an 18-3 whitewash of Birmingham, for whom Wally Lloyd was an outstanding if not a prolific scorer. The most notable feature of this meeting was the performance of Cyril Anderson, who on a powdery track proved that he had tremendous potential. A contemporary reporter was highly impressed with the Australian's performance: 'Cyril invariably does a great speed burst to the first corner, where he broadsides sharply after the fashion of Ron Johnson, and shooting away into the lead, to which he clings tenaciously. His only fault is that he is inclined to slide to earth very frequently.'

This was highlighted in his match race with the Belle Vue star, Arthur Franklyn. Anderson fell three times at the first corner leaving Franklyn to win at the fourth attempt.

Anderson hailed from Toowomba where he had started riding in company with Jack Bishop, his firm friend. Tragically both would be lost to the sport within a few years. Anderson was killed in a track crash and Bishop died of TB.

Exeter lost their proud unbeaten record on Friday 30 August when they were beaten 15-6 away at West Ham. This was no disgrace as the Custom House team at that time boasted a powerful line-up which included Sprouts Elder, Ivor Creek and Tiger Sanderson.

Fri   30/8

The next evening Exeter returned to the County Ground where they completed the double over Southampton, despite being without the services of Noel Johnson, the captain, who was fulfilling a previous engagement at the Leicester Super Speedway, and Harold Stevens who was still injured.

Sat   31/8

Jack Bishop was his usual model of consistency leading the first heat from start to finish. His partner Bert Spencer was just beaten for second place by Clarry Eldridge while Eric Lister brought up the rear. Buster Buckland added four more points to the Exeter total when he won heat 2. Behind him another thrilling duel resulted in second place for Southampton's Vic Collins, who narrowly beat Ron Stokes to the line. The other Southampton rider Tommy Cullis fell.

Bishop had everything his own way again in the third heat which he won in a time of 84.2 seconds. Collins kept Buckland in third place to make the final result Exeter 15 Southampton 8.

Luck was with Bishop when he ran into problems during the second heat of the Exeter Handicap. He was speeding down the back straight when without warning his rear wheel collapsed completely. By skilful riding he was able to bring his machine to a halt on the grass without injury to himself. However he made up for this set back by winning the Chevrolet Gold Cup scratch race final in the fastest time of the evening 82.8.

Fred Hawken showed considerable improvement to win the handicap final, but much interest was aroused by Southampton newcomer Tommy Cullis, who managed to gain third place in each of the finals, his efforts being nothing if not spectacular. In his scratch semi-final Cullis' front tyre burst as he approached the finish line and his machine ran out of control across the track. Happily the rider, who was thrown, landed without injury on the grass where he was awarded second place behind Lew Lancaster.

Tues 3/9 The third Revel took place on Tuesday 3 September. Unfortunately several of the top stars who had been booked were unable through injury to take part, but their replacements still provided plenty of thrills. Jack Bishop, now billed as the Exeter Champion, won the Hospital Cup donated by Sir Edgar Plummer, president of the R.D.& E. Hospital. The cup was presented to Bishop by the injured Harold Stevens. Lew Lancaster won the £10 first prize for the Exeter Handicap.

The thrill of the evening came in the first semi-final of the Flying 12 Scratch Race. First away was Ivor Creek closely followed by Ron Stokes, Buster Buckland and 'Dusty' Haig. They continued in close formation until the third bend of the last lap when Stokes fell. Buckland then made a super-human effort around the outside but in doing so collided wtih Creek and lost control. The two machines crossed the line locked together. Creek made a desperate effort to part them and swerved away. This caused Buckland to be thrown from his Douglas. The machine tore on down the straight and crashed into the safety fence. Creek helped Buckland to his feet and was declared the winner.

Despite the efforts of Lew Lancaster Exeter easily beat Coventry, at that time second in the speedway League, by 17-4 in an inter city match. Bishop and Buckland scored maximum points over Lancaster in heat 1. Noel Johnson and Bert Spencer produced a repeat performance in heat 2 when they headed George Allbrook home, but Lancaster managed to split Bishop and Johnson in the final. Exeter's victory was particularly sweet for Leonard Glanfield as his brother Stanley was the promoter at Brandon.

Southern Speedways had decided to reintroduce twice weekly meetings starting that Saturday evening. On that occasion it looked as if Jack Bishop's undoubted County Ground supremacy would be challenged when his friend and fellow countryman Cyril Anderson qualified for the final of the Silver Helmet. Anderson had shown great form all evening and in the scratch semi-final had actually beaten Bishop in 82.6 seconds, exactly the same time as Bishop had recorded when they had met in an earlier qualifying heat. However the fans were deprived of seeing the battle for supremacy decided in the final as Bishop was forced out with engine trouble. Anderson had no such difficulty and won easily from Ron Stokes and Noel Johnson. The win raised Anderson to 'star' status. *Sat 7/9*

The Exeter City team gained ample revenge for their defeat in East London the previous week by beating West Ham 13-8. Buckland won the first heat from Bruce McCullum and Tiger Stevenson after Johnson fell on the opening lap. Stokes and Swift headed Buzz Hibberd in heat 2, but Hibberd turned the tables in the final to finish ahead of Buckland and Stokes.

Ivor Creek's evening was spoilt by bad luck and mechanical difficulties, but the West Ham star managed to overcome the gremlins and win the handicap final.

Cyclone Billy Lamont made a welcome reappearance the following Wednesday and proved again to the Exeter fans that dirt track racing was a most exhilarating sport. Lamont took on Bishop in a match race series the decider of which proved most eventful. First the Cyclone's AJS gave problems, then Bishop's Duggie also mysteriously packed up. Lamont's motor picked up and he was soon hammering around again. But just as he was about to catch Bishop the latter's engine burst back into life and the Exeter favourite roared away to win, albeit in a time of 93 seconds. *Wed 11/9*

Jack also held the upper hand in the Gold Sash final where he again beat Billy. The Cyclone had to be content with second place in the handicap final as well. In this one he was unable to catch Buckland who had received a two second start. Buster also retained the Plummer Cup by beating Charlie Swift. The racing chemist had earlier met Stokes in the qualifier, but won easily when Stokes fell.

Jack Barnet, the High Beech star, made an impressive debut on Exeter cinders but both Bert Spencer and Cyril Anderson missed out because of machine problems.

Sat 14/9 No foreigners were present this Saturday but that was made up for by the splendid riding of the locals. The main feature involved attempts on the track record. Although none were actually broken Bert Spencer won a magnificent silver model yacht presented by Leonard Glanfield for recording the fastest single lap. Spencer, Buckland and Bishop had all tied with times of 19.6 seconds. In the run-off Spencer clocked 19.8, Bishop 20.0, and Buckland 20.4.

Lew Lancaster won the Cottey Cup for the quickest four laps with a time of 76.6 seconds.

Fred Hawken who was in fine form won the Exeter Handicap. Given a three second start, he raced away and finished with time in hand.

Jack Bishop added another trophy to his already impressive collection when he won the Silver Star scratch final. Bishop made a good start and won comfortably from Charlie Swift, but shortly after crossing the finish line snapped a chain.

Wed 18/9 Leonard Glanfield found himself very much up against it the following Wednesday. Wizard Frank Arthur had been booked to appear, but had crashed during a meeting in London earlier in the week so was forced to withdraw. This left Glanfield with very little time to find a suitable replacement, and the telephone in the Southern Speedways office worked overtime. Eventually Harry Taft of Birmingham agreed to help out. As it was already afternoon arrangements were put in hand to fly Taft down, but these failed to materialize and instead the next best thing was to drive down. It was reported that "A fast moving motor was requisitioned. Taft's racing machine was strapped up behind and he came along, reaching the Exeter track at just after nine p.m."

This was Taft's first visit to the County Ground, and after a couple of practice laps he lined up against Buckland and Stokes in a heat of the Silver Trophy scratch race. Unfortunately he was passed by Stokes and failed to reach the semi-final. In his match race with Bishop the Birmingham rider's machine failed, so Taft had little to show for his efforts, although the crowd were not slow to show their appreciation.

Sadly the crowd was a mere 4,000, the smallest seen since the introduction of the speedway and a thousand down on the previous Saturday. Prior to Taft's arrival Glanfield had leaflets printed and handed out to the public before they entered the stadium. These explained the situation and also why Arthur would not be appearing. While this gesture was greatly appreciated by the public, whose sympathy was obviously with Glanfield, many chose not to pay to go into the meeting.

Despite the difficulties the racing was exceptionally good and the programme interesting. Instead of the much published head to head races between the local stars and Frank Arthur, a knockout competition between Bishop, Lancaster, Buckland and Spencer was introduced. The winner was Bishop who made the fastest time of the evening in his match race with Buckland.

The Silver Trophy scratch final produced an excellent race which was fought out by Bishop, Cyril Anderson, Buckland and Stokes. They all got away to a good start but it was Bishop who led around the first bend with Anderson sitting on his tail. On the third lap Anderson went through and holding the inside line won by three yards. It was a popular win and Anderson received his trophy from Lady Elizabeth Hare, daughter of the Earl of Listowel.

Lew Lancaster won the handicap event, and it was noted that there was a great improvement in the order of the track. Grading at the start of the season was undertaken by an ancient gentleman who drove an equally ancient

Sunbeam motor car which towed the chain drags. He was nicknamed Major Seagrave after the current World Speed record holder. The Sunbeam was later replaced by a Chevrolet truck supplied by Reid & Lee.

Sat 21/9 The locals were again left to provide the thrills on the Saturday evening. 17 year old Bert Spencer, the Baby Cyclone as he was known by his Exeter fans, looked set to take the double. Spencer rode magnificently throughout and confidently won the Gold Gauntlet final despite being harried all the way by Frank Buckland. Alas Bert missed out in the Exeter Handicap when, after another good start, he was forced out with machine problems.

Buckland defended his Plummer Cup, easily defeating Reg Beer who had earlier beaten Kirk. Happy sustained facial injuries when he crashed in the main event but the damage was not serious.

Alas on the same evening a far more tragic accident took place at the Leicester Super Speedway which resulted in the death of popular Torquay rider Roy Reeves. Roy, who had joined Leicester Super a couple of months previously, was running second to Arthur Sherlock in heat 1 of the handicap event. Half way round Reeves fell. Third place man A. Bowering managed to pass between the fallen rider and his machine, but R. F. Christian who was following close behind and whose view was obstructed, ran into Reeve and was thrown.

It was evident that Roy had been badly injured and it was soon announced that he was dead. The crowd of 30,000 stood bare-headed for a moment then quietly dispersed. It transpired later that Reeves' helmet had been smashed and that he had received terrible injuries.

The funeral took place at Roy's home village of Modbury with a large turn out of local speedway personalities present. There were also floral tributes from Exeter Speedway, (in the shape of the club badge,) Wimbledon, Nottingham, Leicester Super and Leicester Stadium Speedways, Wembley and the Northern Dirt Track Association.

This tragic event started a spate of strange stories and soon afterwards the Leicester Mail reported that the spirit

LEONARD GLANFIELD,
the man who introduced
speedway to Exeter.

FREDDIE HORE,
the first man to ride the
Exeter track.

Leonard Glanfield with his riders. L to R. Jack Bishop, Frank Buckland, Ron Stokes, Leonard Glanfield, Noel Johnson, Harold Stevens, Bert Spencer.

Leonard Glanfield welcomes riders at St. Davids Station before the first Speedway Revel 25 June 1929. L to R. L. Glanfield, Vic Huxley, Eric Spencer, Stan Spencer, Billy Lamont, Frank Arthur, Dicky Case.

WIZARD
FRANK ARTHUR
on his Harley
Davidson
'Peashooter'
machine.

H. STEVENS and C. SWIFT indulging in a tear up.

HAROLD STEVENS.

FRANK 'BUSTER'
BUCKLAND.

LIONEL
VAN PRAAG,
Speedway's first
World Champion
1936.

Jack Bishop passing Cecil Brown on the inside, with Frank Arthur overtaking, at
first Revel — note size of crowd.

1929 Exeter team in the County Ground pits. L to R. Ron Stokes, Frank Buckland, Jack Bishop, Noel Johnson and Bert Spencer.

ROY REEVES.

Start of the B Grade scratch race.

Getting away at Exeter. Noel Johnson, Buster Buckland and Happy Kirk
revving-up in a heat in the Gold Helmet scratch race

RON JOHNSON and FRED MOCKFORD.

'BUGGIE'
FLEEMAN.

A typically harmless fall, with a rider sliding to earth to avoid the other.

RICHARD FLEEMAN with the author at the County Ground 1989.

COLIN WATSON.

Pits scene on opening night 1934. L to R. Gordon Taylor, unknown, Broncho Slade, kneeling Freddie Hawken, Reg Beer (against post), Bill Knowles, Arthur Millett.

The line up for the Southern Championship August 1945. L to R. Back: Jack Parker, Ron Clark, Oliver Hart, Mike Erskine, Fred Tuck.
Front: Wally Lloyd, Ron Johnson, Colin Watson, Bill Kitchen, Eric Chitty.

Winner BILL KITCHEN with the trophy.

BLUEY WILKINSON
World Champion 1938.

Crash at Alphington 1945.

HARRY 'HAPPY' KIRK.

RON STOKES.

BERT SPENCER.

CHARLIE SWIFT.

NOEL JOHNSON.

JACK BISHOP.

of the unfortunate Reeves had appeared to his widow when she visited the Super track. The story went that a mysterious something compelled Mrs Reeves to walk around the track. She was accompanied by Roy's friend Cyril Hefford and two mechanics Sid Rumbsey and Sid Heather. When they reached the fatal spot Mrs Reeves declared that her husband appeared to her and spoke words, some far too sacred to be revealed. Among the things he said was that he wished one of his medals to be worn by his widow, another by his mother and a third buried with him.

Cyril Hefford, Roy's chum, who was said not to be an imaginative person, declared that he saw the apparition, and so did the two mechanics, although none of them heard what was said. Reeves was dressed in his track riding attire and wore a crash helmet.

Sid Heather told a reporter: "We were walking round the track when we suddenly stiffened. It was an eerie feeling. At that moment I seemed to see Roy." Another mechanic explained that they had looked round and seen a man leaning against the barrier sobbing. It was pointed out that Reeves had been credited with psychic powers since he was four years old.

The Leicester Mercury on the same day made the statement that Mrs Reeves, who was not yet 20 years old, hoped to take up dirt track racing as a profession.

Back at the County Ground Leonard Glanfield was *Wed 25/9* hoping that the problems created by falling crowds and the lack of 'crack' riders would be rectified by a good attendance at the fourth Revel which was scheduled for Wednesday 25 September. Unfortunately problems continued to arise. First Frank Arthur was still unfit and therefore unable to ride. Then his replacement Geoff Taylor along with Max Grosskreutz ran into trouble on the way down.

It appears that the two Australians were driving fairly quickly in a bid to get to the County ground in time for the 7.45 pm start. Near Yeovil another road user complained to the police about a car being driven 'at express speed'.

They contacted Honiton Police Station by telephone but not quickly enough, as the car, complete with trailer carrying the two 'speed irons', had already gone through. Constables Rice and Pike of Honiton immediately commandeered a car and gave chase, but were unable to close the gap.

The chase continued all along the 17 miles to Exeter but as Grosskreutz and Taylor arrived in High St the city force who had received a telephone call from Honiton stopped them outside the Express & Echo offices. A crowd quickly gathered when it was realised that they were two speedway stars en route to the track. While the police sorted the matter out, word was sent to the County Ground that they had been delayed. The crowd were told that the two riders had been held up by Exeter Police for furious driving, but would be along in a few minutes. The crowd, it was reported, were 'rather tickled at the furious driving business, and seemed to take Mr Parkes' announcement in the light of a joke'. It certainly turned out to be no joke for Max and Geoff, but their late arrival was greeted with cheers.

Alas Grosskreutz and Taylor did not arrive at the track until 9.00pm which meant that several races had to be rescheduled. Happily the prospect of an all star field had attracted a 12,000 crowd which must have offset some of Mr Glanfield's worries, while the racing also lived up to the billing.

Local riders dominated the Exeter Handicap. Spencer, Lancaster, Stokes and Swift fought it out in the final, with the latter leading all the way.

Wizard Frank Arthur made a personal appearance and told the crowd via the PA of his elbow injury. It was rather smugly reported that "his few sentences over the microphone, although somewhat disjointed — Arthur does not aspire to oratorical eminence — were appreciated by the crowd who cheered when the Wizard announced that he hoped to participate in more than one Exeter meeting before the season closed."

The final of the Chevrolet Gold cup, generously donated

by Messrs. Reid & Lee, Motor Engineers, was won by Harold Stevens, after Bishop had crashed heavily. Jack had shot away at the start but ran wide on the banking and fell. He was carried from the track badly shaken, and took no further part in the evenings activities. Stevens rode with considerable dash considering that it was his first appearance since breaking his ribs in the crash at Southampton. Although sternly chased by Anderson and Buckland he maintained his lead and the crowd rose as one when he crossed the finish line. Arthur was on hand to present him with the trophy.

The highspot of the meeting was the All Star Scratch Race. Heat 1 of which was a desperate encounter between Vic Huxley, Ivor Creek, Geoff Taylor and Bishop, which ended with Huxley narrowly getting the better of the local rider. Jack Barnett, the High Beech star, beat Billy Lamont in heat 2 after Stevens had fallen while leading and Grosskreutz had run into machine problems. The final proved to be a procession with Lamont, aboard Arthur's Harley Peashooter, winning easily from Huxley.

Unfortunately the meeting had become very drawn out and did not finish until 10.40pm. This was because the Taylor/Grosskreutz affair necessitated the re-arranging of a number of heats and further delays were caused by false starts and long waits while riders came to the start. An extra half hour delay occurred when a collection was taken up for Roy Reeves' widow. Nobody begrudged this as the riders diligently covered all parts of the ground, but the lateness of the hour meant that there was less time to tread the light fantastic at the Revel Dance which took place at the Rougemont Hotel afterwards.

This again proved a huge success with dancing taking place to Len Taylor, Exeter's Red Demon of the Piano. Speedway announcer Paddy Parkes took command of the drums and announced Harold Stevens, the hero of the evening, who with his wife led off the foxtrot.

The attendance was disappointing again the following *Wed 2/10* Wednesday when only an estimated crowd of around 3,000 turned up for what was a good programme. Stevens took the top honour, the Silver Star, after a grim struggle with Buckland. Bishop and the ever popular Lew Lancaster both suffered plenty of ill luck. Bishop's machine packed up twice, while Lancaster had his frame and chain snap when way out in front during his scratch race heat. Earlier Lew had equalled the 79.4 flying four lap track record, a speed of 43 mph.

Another new star emerged that evening. She was Dorothy Bunt from Delabole in Cornwall. In her first public appearance Dorothy was matched against the redoubtable Fay Taylour. Although Dorothy was given half a lap start, she was good enough to hold on to it, even though her very much more experienced opponent made a great race of it. Fay was not quite able to make up the distance much to the delight of Miss Bunt's trainer, Nick Drake.

A match race between Noel Johnson and Geoff Taylor of Halifax provided the crowd with good entertainment. Taylor led the first leg for three and a half laps on his 'droning' Scott but Noel judged it nicely coming through on the inside to snatch victory a couple of yards from the flag. The Halifax rider seemed to have the second leg in the bag when his chain snapped leaving Johnson to cruise home. By coincidence Noel's chain also broke as he crossed the finish line.

Sat 5/10 The deteriorating situation with the promotion was highlighted by a post match announcement from Glanfield stating that the following Saturday's meeting had been cancelled. The reason for this was stated as being that Frank Arthur was unable to appear as hoped. However the Wizard had accepted a booking for the following Wednesday. To add to the problems complaints had been made to the police from some quarters regarding the influx of traffic for speedway meetings. This was discussed at length by the match committee, with the Chief Constable coming out strongly in favour of the speedway.

Wed 9/10 The last meeting to be held under Leonard Glanfield's Southern Speedways banner took place on Wednesday 9 October, and was marred by a bad smash involving Harold Stevens. Hard luck Harold has been chasing Frank Arthur in the final of the Exeter Trophy scratch race but as he moved to overtake the Wizard he came down and Charlie Swift was unable to avoid him. It was obvious that Stevens had taken a bad one. He was stretchered off and taken to the Royal Devon & Exeter Hospital where he was diagnosed as having fractured his thigh. It was the worst misfortune to befall Harold in what had without doubt been an unlucky season. In the rerun Buckland beat Arthur.

Earlier Jack Bishop had beaten the Wizard in a match race and in doing so had succeeded in equaling the four lap record. Dorothy Bunt achieved another victory this time over Noel Johnson, but it was a somewhat empty achievement as the popular Australian had fallen off.

Two days later came the fateful news. Racing had been suspended and the gates of the County Ground locked. *Fri 11/10* Considerable surprise and disappointment was felt by the fans as another big meeting had been planned to support the forthcoming St. Thomas Carnival which in those days was a major local event. Rumour and speculation were rife as it was common knowledge that another Revel was planned to round off the season. A reporter called at the Southern Speedways Ltd office in High St. twice during the morning in the hope of seeing one of the directors. Calling a third time he found a young lady who confirmed that it had been decided to discontinue meetings immediately. She was unable to say what had led to the decision, only the managing director, Mr Glanfield, or the secretary, Mr Gibbs, were able to do that and they were both out.

A board meeting had been held the day before which had lasted two and a half hours. Although the official attitude of the directors was never disclosed it was clear that it was then that the decision to close had been made.

Mr Jack Coombes, secretary of the Exeter Rugby Club was also interviewed but declined to make a statement, other than to confirm the closure and explain that a meeting of a small sub-committee would take place that evening with the club solicitors.

"The position is not hopeless" he commented. "Perhaps by co-operation between the speedways and the Exeter

Club and others the difficulties may be overcome."

When the riders turned up that morning at the County Ground they found that the groundsman had instructions from the hon. sec. of the Rugby Club to keep the doors locked and allow no one in without special permission. Exceptions were made in some instances where men had left personal kit inside the grounds.

Later Mr F. P. Cottey, solicitor to Southern Speedways, commented on the closure"

"It is correct to say that Southern Speedways Ltd. have decided to cancel their big revels arranged for this month. The strenuous opposition by a certain section of the population of St. Thomas has undoubtedly had a most injurious effect upon the supporters of speedway racing there.

It does not necessarily mean that this is the end of speedway racing in Exeter.

Those connected with more than one of the big speedway tracks in the county have put out feelers regarding the Exeter track."

The sudden stoppage of the speedway continued to be the principal topic of discussion in the city and neighbourhood the next day. There was a consensus of opinion that the stoppage would only be temporary, and that the sport would be restarted, if necessary by another organisation.

An un-named committee member of the Rugby Club was reported by the Express & Echo as saying, "It is too good a thing to be dropped entirely. There is no doubt that speedway in Exeter is a gold mine." He also claimed to have statistics which showed that the attendance had averaged 8,000. The last two meetings had only attracted poor crowds, but he disputed the allegation that this was due to complaints voiced in the City Council of a section of the inhabitants in the vicinity of the ground.

Mr. Cottey was quoted as saying that the directors had not had any further meeting, and there was nothing whatever to add to the statements made the day before.

A meeting of Southern Speedways Ltd. was called for the following Saturday at Bedford Circus, Exeter. The shareholders were very few, and the bulk of the capital was held by the directors.

Afterwards a meeting of the riders was held at their garage in Okehampton St. the following statement was issued:

"A speedway meeting, specially arranged by the riders, will be held on Wednesday evening at such a time as will not interfere with the arrangements of the St. Thomas Carnival Committee. Wednesday's meeting will be held only subject to permission for the use of the ground being received from the existing Company.

This permission is required so that the matter may be correct in all respects.

The Exeter Rugby Club have kindly placed the ground at the disposal of the riders. It must be clearly understood that this meeting has no connection with Southern Speedways.

The financial arrangements for Wednesday's show are being privately borne and ensure that all costs will be met prior to the commencement of the programme."

The meeting was billed to start at 9.00pm after the *Wed 16/10* carnival procession had completed its route. Frank Arthur and Jim Kempster had agreed to appear but due to injury Kempster was replaced by Ray Tauser. Arthur as always proved the big attraction with a crowd of 7,000 there to welcome him. Not surprisingly he swept the board winning both finals and his match race with Tauser in two straight legs. The Wizard was presented with his prizes by local personality 'Artful Thomas'.

The highlight of the evening was a thrilling finish to heat 4 of the scratch race when Buggie Fleeman made a desperate attempt to catch Jack Bishop on the last lap and was rewarded with a dead heat.

All the takings were divided among the riders and Frank Arthur generously gave his services for the cause. Carnival Collectors mingled with the crowd rattling their tins in aid of the Royal Devon and Exeter Hospital.

So Exeter's first speedway season arrived at its conclusion on a somewhat uncertain note. Happily salvation would soon be on hand in the form of Crystal Palace promoters Red Mockford and Cecil Smith.

CHAPTER FOUR

1930 A NEW START

The flamboyant Leonard Glanfield quickly disappeared from the scene. Glanfield had been a colourful local personality. He drove an expensive Klyno motor car, kept a new speedboat at Exmouth, and enjoyed entertaining both local dignitaries and press at formal dinner parties. His successors at the County Ground were a different breed.

Fred Mockford and Cecil Smith were two entrepreneurs who had previously promoted various forms of motorcycle racing through their London Motor Sports company. In 1926 they were invited to organise regular race meetings on a course laid out around the grounds of the Crystal Palace in South London. At that time the Crystal Palace was a vast leisure and sports complex which was enjoyed by thousands of Londoners. 'Path racing' was held once a month in the summer and regularly attracted crowds of over twenty thousand. When speedway arrived in 1928 the Palace management were quick to see the potential and gave Mockford and Smith the go ahead to build a track around the football pitch where the Cup Final had been staged before Wembley had been built. This is now the site of the National Sports Centre athletics stadium. By 1930 Mockford and Smith were also promoting speedway at Perry Bar, Birmingham.

The news that the two London Businessmen were set to reopen Exeter Speedway was welcomed by the public at large, but the small group of opponents who had made trouble with the City Council in 1929 were openly hostile. An injunction was sought to stop the new venture but was overruled. Legal wrangling went on for much of that summer until the opposition was eventually silenced.

The first meeting at Exeter under the new County Speedways banner was planned for Wednesday 9 April 1930. The big attraction for the opening night was to be an appearance by Ron Johnson who had won the main event at the opening meeting twelve months previously. Unfortunately heavy rain throughout the day flooded the track and left the promoters with no alternative but to postpone the meeting until the following evening. The Rugby Club helped out by cancelling their fixture with Wellington planned for that night so that the speedway meeting could go ahead. *Wed 9/4*

When the racing did get underway twenty four hours later it was soon noted that changes had been made for the better. The organisation had been tightened up and the gaps between races were considerably shorter. There was much less time wasting and the riders were dispatched smartly from the pits. Further time was saved by the riders in the 'flying start' races being pushed off from the pits rather than wheeling their machines around to the start and being fired up from there. The white coats of the 'pushers-off' had also been exchanged for red and white hooped jerseys, the colour of the Exeter City Speedway Team. Another innovation was the American cloth vests worn by the riders over their leathers. This material showed up clearly enabling the spectators to distinguish the riders much more easily. *Thur 10/4*

It was a good start for the new regime with plenty of exciting racing. The match races between Ron Johnson (Crystal Palace) and Noel Johnson (Exeter) proved to be the highlight of the evening. The two Australians, it was reported, shifted the cinders with good effect, but Ron won in two straight runs. He also won the scratch race final. Jack Addison won the handicap final.

Another interesting feature was an international event in which Charlie Swift and Reg Beer took on two Danish riders, Walter Ryle and Kai Anderson. Swift defeated

Anderson in the opening heat while Beer beat Ryle in the second, before going on to take the final from Swift.

Wed 16/4   Press relations must have fallen down on 16 April for there are no reports of the visit of Coventry however the Auto Motor Journal for 25 April 1930 carried a brief match report. Coventry were represented by County Ground favourite Lew Lancaster, Jack and Norman Parker, Tom Farndon, Wilmot Evans and George Allbrook. After a series of thrilling races, the Midlanders secured a narrow victory by 23-28 thanks to the splendid riding of Jack Parker who managed to pull the match out of the fire for Coventry.

Also on the programme was a special match race between the reigning Star Home Riders Champion, Roger Frogley and the runner up Jack Parker. Parker won in two straight runs as Frogley experienced engine trouble.

The following evening the Exeter City team travelled to Brandon for the return match, but cold winds accompanied by rain and hail, made conditions generally unpleasant. It was not a good evening for Exeter as they ended up on the wrong end of a 45-9 whitewash.

Exeter meetings were well publicised at this time and the local papers carried large advertisements detailing the riders taking part. Admission charges in 1930 were 1/2d or 1/10d for the enclosure or 6d for children while grandstand seats cost 3/6d and 2/4d. A footnote stated NO CHANGE GIVEN AT TURNSTILES.

Wed 23/4   The West Ham team visited the County Ground on Wednesday. The star packed Hammers were much too strong for the locals who found themselves on the wrong end of a 30-22 defeat. While Exeter now relied on local talent, rather than Aussies as in '29, West Ham included Tiger Stevenson and future World Champion Bluey Wilkinson in their line-up. Buster Buckland and Charlie Swift rode well for Exeter but the second strings found it tough going, as the Hammers were particularly skilful in preventing their opponents from overtaking. The scorers were Exeter: Buckland 8, Swift 8, Kirk 5, Addison 1. West Ham: Arthur Westwood 6, Don Durrant 6 + 1, Bluey Wilkinson 5 + 2, Den Taylor 5 + 1, Tiger Stevenson 5, Les Maguire 3.

Stevenson gave the Hammers their second victory of the evening when he beat Swift in two straight legs of their match race, although in the third leg Stevenson fell and Swift damaged the forks on his machine when laying down to avoid the prostrate Hammer.

Jack Addison took advantage of a favourable handicap to win the final of that event from Reg Beer, Buckland and Swift. Addison was away and gone, but the other three battled it out every inch of the way. Buckland was unlucky to be beaten from scratch while Swift broke his chain in the last few yards.

Wed 30/4

Cardiff produced a thrilling match when they raced at Exeter the following week. The excitement was maintained right up to the last lap of the final heat. Engine troubles had plagued the Exeter riders throughout the evening, even though Buckland beat Luke by a wheel in one thrilling race. With both sides level on 24 points a piece, everything depended on that last heat. Noel Johnson, brought in to strengthen the Exeter team, and Happy Kirk lined up for the home side while the Cardiff pair were John Wade and Charlie 'Champ' Upham. Johnson took an immediate lead but was forced to retire when his engine failed. This left the Welshmen in Control. Although Kirk was close behind he could not find an opening until the last lap when he darted through to win and force the draw. This saved Exeter from their fourth consecutive inter-track defeat.

The scorers were Exeter: Swift 9, Buckland 6, Kirk 5, Johnson 4, Beer 2, Addison 1. Cardiff: Jack Luke 7, John Wade 5 + 1, Taffy Williams 5 + 1, Will Hopkins 4 + 1, Charlie Upham 4, Fred Hampson 2 + 1.

Jack Luke gained his revenge by beating Buckland 2-0 in the match race, while Reg Beer won the handicap final from Swift.

Wed 7/5

There was disappointment as well as thrills the next week when it was announced that Ron Johnson had not arrived. 'Johnno' was due to have taken part in the International "Big 6" contest. This was eventually won by Noel Johnson who had just fitted a new engine in his Bitzer machine. In the qualifying rounds Buckland finished alone when Swift fell in heat 1. The Tiverton chemist had been chasing Buster hard but as he endeavoured to go down the inside of his Exeter rival Charlie came a purler. Although he avoided landing on his head, he hurt his thumb badly. Reg Beer beat the Australian Harold Hastings in heat 2 while Johnson himself defeated Triss Sharp (England) in the third. The final saw Johnson finish ahead of Buckland and Beer.

The diminutive Exeter skipper however had to accept second place behind Joe Francis (Crystal Palace) in the close fought final of the Devon Scratch Race. Frank Jarman won the Exeter Handicap from Shep Shepherd.

There were several spills and three Exeter riders were injured.In the handicap final Happy Kirk was lying second when he appeared to get into a speed wobble and crashed. Jack Addison could not avoid him and also came down. Both were carried off, and Kirk was taken to hospital suffering from concussion, a gash in the ribs and a badly cut hand. Swift had, as previously mentioned, damaged his thumb in the "Big 6" contest.

Wed 14/5   Jack Ormiston and Colin Watson of Wembley were the main attraction at the meeting which took place on Wednesday 14 May. Ormiston came out on top in both the "British Star 4" and the "Flying 9" scratch race. These two top riders also set some of the fastest times of the season so far, and rather overawed the locals. Watson beat Swift by over half a lap in their heat of the 'Star 4', and his winning time of 78.8 seconds was very quick considering the bumpy state of the track.

Watson also appeared somewhat overawed by his teammate in the final. Ormiston appeared to combine some of Watson's steadiness with the recklessness of a 'Billy Lamont' and won despite breaking a pinion in his gearbox during the last lap. Ormiston repeated his victory in the final of the 'Flying 9'.

Noel Johnson suffered a bout of engine trouble and this cost him the final of the Exeter Handicap which was instead won by Buckland. Buster, it was reported, showed a tendency to ride too wide and would have done better to keep to the white line or at least mid track.

A match race between Exeter and South Africa resulted in a win for the homesters. Will Nicholas and Alan Reeve represented the Dominion but were beaten by Addison and Beer respectively, their winning times being 86.7 and 84.4. The two Exeter riders then met in the final with Addison taking the honours.

Wed 21/5

The world famous Wembley Lions made their first ever appearance at the County Ground on 21 May, but were soundly beaten 39-15. This was the Exeter City team's first victory of the year, and in six of the nine heats the local riders took maximum points. Noel Johnson, Reg Beer and Jack Addison were all unbeaten by an opponent while Stan Cattlett was the Lions' sole race winner in heat 1. Buster Buckland was mounted on a new single cylinder Rudge and had to adopt a different style to that which he used for his Douglas.

The Exeter scorers were: Beer 7 + 1, Addison 7 + 1, Stokes 7 + 1, Johnson 6 + 3, Buckland 6, Swift 6. Wembley: Stan Cattlett 5, Bert Fairweather 3, Charlie Barrett 2, Cliff Parkinson 2, Norman Evans 1, Terry White 1, Art Warren 1.

A disappointing feature of the evening which had been thrill packed throughout was the poor form of Billy Lamont. The Cyclone lacked his usual fire and although he was seen on a variety of machinery, including a Rudge, a Douglas and a Blackburne Wallis, he did not have the best of luck. The presence of Ron Johnson however made up for Lamont's off night. The Crystal Palace star was on spectacular form. The little Aussie deemed not to use his 'cutout' to slow down for the bends preferring instead to ride flat out.

Johnson beat Lamont in two straight legs of their match race. Johnno's winning time in the second leg was 79.8 seconds even though the track was 'clink', in a dry and dusty state. He was at his exciting best in the semi final of the Exeter Handicap in which five riders faced the starter.

Reg Robins, from Dunkeswell near Honiton, was the first away, seven seconds in front of Johnson. When flagged off Johnson rocketed after the rest of the field and picked his way through to win the race by inches from Reg Beer and Cliff Parkinson of Wembley who was riding in only his third meeting.

The final was equally thrilling, with Beer managing to hold off Johnson for three laps until the Crystal Palace 'Glazier' squeezed through a gap to win.

The meeting was run off in slick fashion with the minimum of delays, and the handicapping in particular was well organised. The attendance was equally gratifying with between eight and nine thousand fans making it the best crowd of the season so far.

Wed 28/5   Obviously those fans were well pleased with what they saw for they returned in force the following week. Over 9,000 people flocked into the County Ground on Wednesday 28 May where as always the prospect of an appearance by the Wizard Frank Arthur had proved a major attraction, especially when he was billed to compete against Ron Johnson.

In the event Johnson was not on such good form as the previous week and the 'Wizard' won their match race in two straight legs. The first of these proved to be a neck and neck affair until Johnno's motor faltered slightly. Arthur's winning time was 79.0.

Although Frank won the scratch race final in fine style from Ron Stokes, he was not quite so successful in the handicap final where Frank Jarman made the most of a four second start to notch a notable victory. This was a remarkable achievement for Jarman who had only been racing for five weeks.

Various record attempts were made but although none were broken, Buster Buckland established a new standing start four lap record of 88.0 seconds.

19 year old Clem Mitchell, who was attached to Crystal Palace, made a favourable first impression with the Exeter fans.

With the crowds on the up and up, promoter Fred Mockford took the opportunity to appeal for fair play from the local opponents of Exeter Speedway. He claimed that rumours were being spread by busybodies who wished to stop speedway racing in Exeter. A consequence of these rumours was that people who lived in outlying areas believed the track to be already closed down. Mockford instanced the fact that a charabanc proprietor at Okehampton, who usually conveyed three coach loads to every meeting, had only brought one to this particular meeting. As the livelihood of 2,000 riders throughout the country depended on speedway, Mockford considered that there should be fair play.

There is no doubt that there was venomous opposition to the sport in the city at this time. My father, long time supporter and track manager Ted Lethbridge recalls that around this time the minister of the Church Road Chapel, which was later taken over by the Salvation Army before more recently becoming the Exeter Shotokan Karate Club, had got up a petition to get the speedway closed. Ted, a schoolboy at the time, clearly remembers how cross he was when he discovered that his grandmother had been inveigled into signing the petition by the interfering minister.

Despite the opposition the racing on 4 June produced *Wed 4/6* plenty of thrills although former Exeter favourite Harold Stevens, now based at Leicester and making his first County Ground appearance of 1930, proved once again that he was aptly nicknamed. After going fairly well in the early stages Stevens' evening was spoilt by a number of engine failures and broken chains.

In fact it was a broken chain on Stevens' machine which cost the Colonies victory over the Homeland in a four heat international team match. The Colonies led 8-10 going into the last heat after Buckland and Stokes had collided on the run in of heat 3. When Stevens' chain snapped it allowed Charlie Swift and Wally Lloyd to take a 5-1 over Alan Reeve thus allowing Exeter to clinch victory.

The fourth heat of the Exeter Handicap produced a spectacular crash on the home straight. Alan Reeve wobbled and Stokes crashed into him. Both machines were badly damaged while Reeve sustained slight concussion and ankle injuries. Stokes escaped with a shaking.

Wembley star Colin Watson provided the greatest number *Wed 11/6* of thrills at the following week's meeting, when the main feature was a match race series between Australia, England and New Zealand. Watson first beat former Exeter rider Bert Spencer, who had also moved to Leicester, before going on to defeat New Zealand Champion, Wally Kilminster, who had previously knocked out Buster Buckland. Watson also went on to win the scratch race final in the record race time of 78.8 seconds. The outright flying start record of 76.4 still stood to the credit of Billy Lamont who had set the time in a special attempt staged the previous season.

To round off a highly successful evening Watson completed the treble by coming from the back to win the handicap final after conceding 2 second starts to Frank Jarman, Freddie Hawken and Reg Beer.

A new innovation was a series of inter-track match races against Wolverhampton. In the opening heat Tommy Deadman beat Dilly Gittins for the honour of representing the Wolves in the final, where he in turn was beaten by Exeter's Reg Beer. Beer having previously defeated Jack Addison in the local heat. Addison had provided a great deal of excitement in an earlier race when his motor caught fire. Bert Spencer had also caused a stir by broadsiding at such an angle that his handlebars actually touched the track. Amazingly he managed to recover and continue the race.

Wed 18/6   A 'Star Six Contest' topped the bill on Wednesday 18 June with Jim Kempster (Wimbledon), Squib Burton (Leicester), and George Greenwood (Wembley) matched against the Exeter trio of Noel Johnson, Buster Buckland and Charlie Swift. Swift got Exeter off to a flying start mounted on his new Rudge, and showed that he was now a hard rider to beat around the County Ground by heading home Kempster in the opening heat. Greenwood vanquished Johnson in the second race, while Burton was the victor in heat 3 when Buckland fell.

Local juniors Jack Bingley and Ronald Coleman did well to finish first and second in the Exeter Handicap. Of the 'cracks' Kempster was disappointing but Burton's broadsiding was impressive. The entire meeting was concluded in just an hour and forty minutes.

The Exeter City team gained rapid revenge for their 42-15 defeat at Knowle Park the previous evening when they defeated Bristol 40-13 at the County Ground on 25 June. A bone of contention in the team match was the fact that the ACU referee 'did not seem to notice that the majority of the Bristol men broke the rules by dispensing with goggles'.

Buckland had an unusually bad meeting. After suffering engine trouble several times, Buster took a heavy tumble. Having got into a tremendous speed wobble his machine slewed across the track. The front wheel hit the safety fence and smashed away the top portion. The machine was catapulted up into the air with the rider before crashing back onto the track with Buckland trapped beneath. Happily the Exeter skipper soon rose smiling with only cuts to his face to show for his adventure. Reg Beer meanwhile had laid down his machine in avoiding action.

In the ladies event Miss Sunny Somerset, from London, was soundly beaten by Dorothy Bunt in a time of 99.5 seconds.

CHAPTER FIVE

1930 STEADY PROGRESS

Wed 2/7   The Exeter Track Championship was introduced on 2 July. This involved all the locally based riders. The new championship was intended to be run as an on going series of regular match races. Exeter's pool of riders eligible to take part at this time was made up of Noel Johnson, Frank Buckland, Charlie Swift, Ron Stokes, Freddie Hawken, Jack Addison, Reg Beer, Jack Bingley and Frank Jarman.

The first round was between Stokes and Beer, the latter winning in two straight legs which included an amazing run around the boards.

Heavy rain during the day had threatened to spoil this meeting, but the weather fortunately improved shortly before start time. The track however was left in an extremely slippery state and some hectic action was witnessed. Colin Watson narrowly missed out in his attempts on both track records. The Wembley man clocked 18.9 seconds for .the one lap and 76.6 for the flying four laps, as against Frank Arthur's 18.4 and Billy Lamont's 76.4.

The match race between Watson and Ron Johnson produced a terrific sudden death affair. From the flag both riders hurtled around wheel to wheel until Johnno's chain snapped under the strain. In the rerun which took place later in the evening Johnson led for three laps before Watson sneaked through on the straight.

The two 'cracks' met again in both the major finals.

Although Johnson took his revenge in the scratch event, more engine trouble cost him the handicap which was duly won by Watson.

A team match against Crystal Palace thrilled the patrons *Wed 9/7* the following week. Palace riders had been regular visitors to the County Ground all season as the Sudenham track also came under the promotional banner of Mockford and Smith. However the Glaziers first full team appearance was hampered by engine failures suffered by Ron Johnson and Joe Francis. Exeter meanwhile were without their Aussie skipper Noel Johnson who was nursing a foot injury.

The nine heats were closely contested and Ron Johnson in particular made the cinders fly whenever he was on track. It was not until heat 7 that Exeter took the lead after just one point had separated the two teams for 4 heats. Bad luck for the visitors spoilt what was otherwise a good match which Exeter won by 29-24. Joe Francis, Wally Lloyd and Alan Reeve were all race winners for Crystal Palace.

Ronald Coleman finished ahead of Reeve in the handicap final after both Buckland and Johnson had been forced out by engine trouble. Frank Jarman beat Freddie Hawken in the second round of the track championship.

In the absence of regular announcer Paddy Parkes, Fred Mockford took over the microphone himself and it was noted that he carried out his duties with a dry sense of humour that was much enjoyed by the fans.

The Southampton team was billed to appear on 16 July *Wed 16/7* but due to a rearranged league fixture their visit had to be postponed. Instead a 'Flying 6' event was staged at short notice, featuring Belle Vue Manchester's Ivor Creek, Bert Spencer and Freddie Hore, both of Leicester Super, Joe Francis (Crystal Palace) and Exeter riders Frank Buckland and Charlie Swift.

Creek saw off Buckland in the first heat, Swift beat Spencer in the second while Francis headed home Hore in the third. Creek won the final with Swift second.

The Belle Vue star also won the scratch final from Reg Beer who in turn beat Freddie Hawken and Reg Robins in the junior handicap event. There were frequent spills, one of which ruled Jack Bingley out of the decider of his Track Championship qualifier against Jack Addison.

Noel Johnson winded himself when he collided with the safety fence and it was later discovered that he had broken his collarbone.

Wed 23/7   Southampton made a belated appearance for a South Coast Championship match on 23 July. The Saints who included Geoff Taylor and Australian star Arnie Hansen were in consistent form winning by 21½-31½, the dead heat coming in heat 6 when Buckland and Ken Purser tied for second place. Purser, who had been popular with Exeter fans the previous year, received a rousing cheer when he laid his machine down to avoid the fallen Charlie Swift.

Frank Buckland took over the Exeter captaincy, as Noel Johnson was still injured, and got the locals off to an excellent start when he finished ahead of Taylor in the first heat. However the Saints proved to be the best team seen so far and romped to a comfortable win. The scorers were Exeter: Buckland 7½, Swift 4, Hawken 4 + 2, Addison 2, Stokes 2, Beer 2. Southampton: Arnie Hansen 9, Geoff Taylor 8, Frank Goulden 5, Eric Lister 5, Ken Purser 3½ + 1, Jimmy Hayes 1.

The meeting was drawn out due to a great number of false starts and difficulties in getting machines started so the racing was not concluded until 10pm by which time a number of spectators had already left.

Wed 30/7   The Exeter management designated the following week's speedway as the Great Victory Meeting following Mockford and Smith's success over the legal injunction in the law courts. To celebrate a whole host of top riders had been booked in for what looked like being the best field since the inception of the sport in Exeter. Unfortunately several of those top riders, namely Colin Watson, Ormiston and Wally Lloyd, had to withdraw because of injury. They were replaced by Ivor Creek, Shep Shepherd and Harry Taft, while other visitors included Harry Whitfield (Wembley), Wally Kilminster and Joe Francis. The crowd, which was larger than usual, saw a meeting which one reporter described as "without hesitation the finest racing ever seen at Exeter. The racing was so close that rider after rider seemed bound to come to grief in the terrific struggles for supremacy." Buster Buckland was responsible for many of those thrills as he battled his way through to three finals.

Buckland was the victor in the 'Big Six Contest' ahead of Taft and Creek. He was third in the handicap event when mounted on his reserve machine behind Jack Addison and Joe Francis who finished literally inches apart. For the scratch final Buster borrowed Wally Kilminster's machine but unfortunately the motor seized. Both Buckland and Francis came to grief while making record attempts, however the local man did manage to lower the standing start record to 81.6 in heat 3 of the handicap.

The meeting was again hampered by the number of false starts, with no less than four in one heat with the same rider being responsible each time.

Portsmouth provided little opposition in the South Coast *Wed 6/8* Championship match on Wednesday 6 August. 'Tiger' Hart, the Portsmouth skipper, was the best rider in a team which did not manage to win a single heat. Exeter won 44-10 with Buckland and new signing Clem Mitchell excelling.

This meeting seems to have been more notable for the number of crashes rather than for good racing. Rex Stoodley was carried off after injuring his leg in a simple fall, then Mitchell and Jack Bingley touched handlebars while racing neck and neck down the straight. Both riders fell. Bingley was able to get up and walk away, but Mitchell, although not seriously hurt was stretchered off. Meanwhile a lady spectator, seemingly overcome by the crash, fainted and had to be carried from the grandstand. These events culminated in the Devon and Exeter Gazette headlining in their match report: HARD KNOCKS — SEVERAL CRASHES AT EXETER SPEEDWAY — LADY SPECTATOR FAINTS.

Injury again robbed the Exeter public of the star attractions *Wed 13/8* on 13 August when Billy Lamont and England captain Jim Kempster were unable to appear. Instead their Wimbledon team-mate, Aussie Dicky Case made an impressive County

Ground debut, while Ray Tauser and Bill Clibbett also helped to fill the gaps in the programme. However it was Buster Buckland who stole the show by beating all the visitors in the 'Big Six Contest'. Unfortunately machine failure precluded him from repeating his success in the scratch final, where Case took the honours from Clibbett and Tauser. The handicap final produced some hair raising action from Tauser and Case, with the latter just managing to take the flag ahead of the American. Buckland meanwhile had to be content with recording the fastest time of the night, 80.1.

Reg Beer won the Track Championship round after losing the first leg to Frank Jarman through engine failure.

Wed 20/8 The following week's meeting had to be abandoned after 12 races due to persistent and drenching rain. Buckland continued his successful run by winning the 'flying 9' final from Jack Luke, and finishing second to Crystal Palace's 'Shep' Shepherd in the handicap final.

Sadly Will Nicholas, the South African rider, was killed in a road accident on Salisbury Plain while on his way home from the meeting, and the crowd observed a minute's silence

Wed 27/8 before the action got underway the next week. On the track the quality of the racing was much improved on that seen over the preceding few weeks. Colin Watson was the star of the evening and by this time the Wembley Lion had become a big favourite with the Exeter fans. Watson distinguished himself on this occasion by winning both the 'Big Six' and the Devon Scratch Race finals in the fast times of 77.6 and 78.0 respectively.

Despite a number of regular star visitors, among them, Jack Orminston, Ron Johnson, Jack Luke, Joe Francis, Shep Shepherd and Hurricane Hampson from Cardiff, it was Frank Buckland who gave Watson a run for his money. After finding the speed to match Johnson, Buckland was unable to maintain the furious pace set by Watson. In the final of the 'Big Six' the Wembley man snatched the lead at the start and won by several lengths.

Frank Jarman took the handicap final from Orminston while Ronald Coleman won the Novices Scratch Race from

Bob Spencer.

Local riders held their own at the next meeting on 3 September, when the programme included several names new to the County Ground. The visitors met with varying success. Harry Taft, although not a newcomer, repeated his success of a few weeks previous by winning the "Flying 9 Contest". Having beaten Bill Clibbett in the first heat Taft lined up against Joe Francis and Clem Mitchell in the final. Both of the Crystal Palace riders fell victim to engine failures and thus Taft finished alone. *Wed 3/9*

George MacKenzie of Edinburgh Marine Gardens was another victim of the gremlins, but Noel Johnson, who had been hoping to do great things with a new engine, fell in the first leg of the Exeter Track Championship and sustained a knee injury.

Buster Buckland rode consistently all evening and was rewarded with victory in the Devon Scratch Race, while the diminutive Ronald Coleman added to his recent successes by winning the handicap final.

Bristol's Ted Bravery proved to be the most successful visitor on Wednesday 10 September. The track was already very wet when racing got underway and as the evening progressed further torrential rain rendered it almost unrideable, but this did not stop Bravery from winning both the handicap and scratch race finals. *Wed 10/9*

The final of the 'Big Six Contest' produced the most thrilling race of the evening. Jack Jackson of Wembley led for two laps but Charlie 'Tiger' Sanderson produced a sudden burst of speed to draw level. These two riders indulged in a neck and neck struggle to the finish with Sanderson crossing the line fractionally ahead. In doing so Sanderson's footrest caught in Jackson's front wheel ripping out the spokes. Fortunately the wheel did not collapse immediately.

Billy Lamont was plagued by engine trouble early on, but when he eventually got his machine going he produced some real 'Cyclone' form. However by this time it was too late for him to reach the main finals.

Reg Robins won the junior event from Will Coleman.

Happily the wet weather failed to spoil the firework display which took place during the interval.

Wed 17/9 The weather was even worse the following week when continuous rain flooded the track by mid-day. Fred Mockford had no choice other than to call off the Open Championship meeting planned for that evening. News of the cancellation was carried in the stop press column of the Express & Echo but even so hundreds of hopeful fans still made their way to the County Ground in the hope that racing would still be able to take place.

Wed 24/9 Fortunately the weather had improved considerably seven days later when Mockford and Smith staged their piece de resistance, an unofficial test match between England and Australia. This was to be the highlight of the 1930 season although unfortunately Wizard Frank Arthur was ruled out as he was confined to bed with internal injuries. Bluey Wilkinson, who went on to become World Champion in 1938, came in to replace him, while Ron Johnson took over as the Aussie skipper.

According to the Express & Echo the test match produced the best racing seen at the track since the introduction of the sport and 'never before has such enthusiasm from a spectators point of view been witnessed'. However there were during the evening a number of false starts and recalls, but this was only to be expected with riders keyed up to do well.

Colin Watson was the captain of England and the Lions also included Tiger Sanderson, Frank Buckland, Harry Taft, Joe Francis, Wally Lloyd and Jack Luke. As well as Johnson and Wilkinson, the Australians were Clem Mitchell, Dicky Case, Noel Johnson, Jack Jackson and Jack Sharpe.

The opening heat produced a classic race. Watson shot away at flag fall closely followed by Ron Johnson. The race developed into a titanic struggle between those two 'cracks', with Watson just managing to keep his nose in front throughout, no matter what Johnno tried. The Aussie skipper made an all out attempt to take the lead on the last bend but the Englishman responded magnificently and won by half a wheel. The packed grandstand came to their feet as one, and the news that Watson had broken the track record by a whole second was well received by the larger than usual crowd. Watson's winning time was 75.4 seconds and Johnson also finished well inside Billy Lamont's long standing 76.4 flying start record.

The second heat also produced hair raising action, when Buckland and Taft lined up against Case and Noel Johnson. The latter unfortunately quickly dropped out with engine failure, as the race became a duel between Buckland and Case. The Australian seemed to be heading for certain victory until Buckland, taking advantage of the banking, burst around the out-side to give England another narrow victory. The margin was again so close that many onlookers believed that it was a dead heat.

After such excitement heat 3 was a somewhat tame affair, and was won easily by Bluey Wilkinson. Wally Lloyd had chased him for three laps until engine trouble had ended his challenge. Watson had an untroubled win in heat 4, while Buckland convincingly defeated Wilkinson in the fifth heat.

Heat 6 provided Australia with their first 5-1 as Ron Johnson roared home ahead of Clem Mitchell to level the scores at 18-18. An engine failure for Watson on the first lap robbed heat 7 of much of its interest, and when Jack Sharpe fell on the second it turned into a match race between Wilkinson and Tiger Sanderson. Wilkinson won putting Australia into a one point lead.

A puncture for Buckland hindered England's chances in the penultimate heat and allowed Ron Johnson and Mitchell to notch up their second 5-1 which put the Aussies firmly in control.

Joe Francis and Wally Lloyd faced Dicky Case and Noel Johnson in the final race, but by the third lap only Francis and Johnson were left. Although the little Aussie hung on grimly his machine was just not quick enough to reduce the gap, and Francis won by several lengths to put the final result at England 24 — Australia 28.

The scratch race did not produce any great excitement.

The England top scorers race turned into a farce when Watson and Buckland dropped out leaving Francis to finish alone. Ron Johnson and Wilkinson fought out a closer affair in the Australian race although Case was forced to pull out. Francis and Johnson met in the final but the Englishman's fly wheel came adrift.

Reg Beer passed Freddie Hawken in the last fifteen yards to win the Exeter Handicap final.

Afterwards Watson issued a challenge to the Australians for a re-match which Mockford hoped to fit in before the season ended.

Wed 1/10 The first evening of October saw Leicester's Squib Burton have a successful time at the County Ground. Squib won two of the three finals and also broke the four lap push start record. His time of 81.1 seconds (42mph) dashed the previous record of 81.6 held jointly by Buckland and Ormiston, and was set in the semi final of the handicap event, where all the riders started from scratch, the first time that this had ever happened at Exeter.

Burton beat Buckland in the final of the 'Big Six Contest' having earlier defeated Lew Lancaster in the first heat. Buckland had qualified by beating Phil Bishop of High Beech in their qualifying heat, while third place man Noel Johnson had disposed of Wilmot Evans.

Coventry's Arthur 'Tiny' Tims won the handicap final from Reg Robins. Buckland retained the Exeter Track Championship when challenger Noel Johnson fell.

Sat 11/10 The Exeter Open Championship, which had been rained off in September, was re-staged on Saturday 11 October. The change of race night was to avoid clashing with the St. Thomas Carnival Procession which traditionally took place on a Wednesday evening.

The £200 Championship proved to be a disappointment due to the fact that no less than seven top riders who, until the last moment had been billed to appear, failed to arrive. It was announced that they were instead riding in a championship meeting in London. Smiling Jim Kempster, who was said to have broken down en route from the capital, as a replacement also failed to put in an appearance.

Lesser riders deputised for the absentees but the racing lacked the kind of thrills expected of a big money championship.

To add to the difficulties several crashes marred the evening's racing. Joe Francis hit the fence and was detained in the Royal Devon and Exeter Hospital with concussion. Dicky Case and Jack Addison both came to grief at the same spot, the former injuring his right foot and the latter suffering facial abrasions.

The Championship was run over six heats, two semis and a match race final in which Ron Johnson beat Phil Bishop to collect the £50 first prize. As one newspaper put it, this may or may not have been compensation for the toe he lost at the County Ground the previous season.

The consolation handicap for those not reaching the scratch final was won by Jack Luke with Noel Johnson second. Freddie Hawken was unlucky to fall when well in the lead.

The grand finale of the 1930 season took place on *Sat 18/10* Saturday 18 October. The England v Australia test match of three weeks before had obviously proved to be such a success that Mockford and Smith decided to round off their first season in charge at the County Ground with a repeat performance. The result of the first match had been a win for the Aussies but this time around the English lads came out on top 30-24.

Colin Watson once again captained the 'England' side which also included Ted Bravery, Frank Buckland, Jack Luke, Jack Ormiston and Phil Bishop, while the Australian line-up consisted of Ron Johnson (captain), Percy Bryant, Charlie Spink, Jack Sharp, Jack Jackson and Noel Johnson. By this time the season was virtually over and many of the other top riders had already sailed for Australia and the season 'Down Under'.

CHAPTER SIX

1931 A SHORT SHARP SEASON

After the problems encountered in 1930 Fred Mockford and Cecil Smith might understandably have decided to move their operation elsewhere. Happily for the Exeter fans they did not, and the new season started with an air of optimism. In the first programme writing under the heading of "Happy Days are Here Again", the promoters had this to say.

'So at last we are together again, having emerged from the gloom of bad weather and other troubles which besought us all last season and now we see glimpses of a silver lining which will, we are certain, with your assistance, spread through the Speedway sky at Exeter and secure for the West the wonderful future for the sport which is rapidly sweeping the Country now'.

'Last year being past, we will let it bury its dead and we hope they will never walk. We are certain that all our Supporters could see the difficulties under which we are labouring and which entirely prevented a constructive season's programme of the best type being put on before you. This year, we are going ahead with our ideas and have fixed up for a wonderful lot of riders to visit you during the coming weeks'.

Thur 14/5 Their aim was fulfilled that very evening when Exeter raced High Beech in the first round of the Daily Mail National Cup Competition. Exeter could not have had tougher opposition for what was their first ever official team fixture.

High Beech were then in the Southern League along with other top teams like Wembley, West Ham, Belle Vue, Crystal Palace and Stamford Bridge. They were known either as the Forresters or the Rabbits and wore colours of Maroon and Cambridge Blue. Their line-up was headed by skipper Syd Edmonds and Jack Barnett, and also included Frank Pearce, Bobby Blake, Billy Dallison, Tiger Hart, Reg Hutchins and Stan Baines. Charles King and Arthur Fenn were the reserves.

The Exeter team included several old favourites plus some new faces. Frank 'Buster' Buckland was once again the captain and was supported by Reg Beer. The ever popular Lew Lancaster was making his first appearance in the Exeter colours of red and white, as were Jack Douglas, Bill Hamblin, Clarrie Eldridge, Doug Hutchins, and Les Maguire. The reserves were Freddie Hawken and Frank Jarman.

The match was staged over 16 heats and various new innovations were introduced. To speed up the proceedings a three minute warning was implemented and the riders were recognised by their helmet colours Red and White for the home riders and Blue and Yellow for the visitors.

Exeter took an early lead when Buckland headed home Syd Edmonds with Reg Beer third, but the Forresters hit back and soon took control of the match, running out easy winners by 34-59. Indeed apart from several drawn heat Exeter's only other heat advantage came in heat 10 when Beer and Frank Jarman sandwiched Tiger Hart for another 4-2. Unfortunately Buckland crashed in heat 5 sustaining concussion and a nasty gash over one eye. Further disaster befell the locals in heat 11 when the Exeter pair crashed with Jack Douglas injuring his leg and Bill Hamblin his shoulder. As a result of these crashes all three riders took no further part in the meeting. Obviously their problems disheartened the Exeter camp for whom Lancaster rode well despite a lack of points.

High Beech were not without their troubles but these were mainly mechanical. Bobby Blake, the young Aussie who had only arrived in England the week before, made the fastest time of the night and both he and Edmonds scored three wins each.

The heat details were as follows:

Ht.	1 Buckland, Edmonds, Beer, Pearce	81.0
Ht.	2 Blake, Douglas, Barnett, Hamblin	82.3
Ht.	3 Dallison, Hart, Eldridge, Hutchins	86.0
Ht.	4 Hutchins, Lancaster, Maguire, Baines	85.8
Ht.	5 Blake, Beer, Barnett, Buckland fell	86.0
Ht.	6 Dallison, Douglas, Hamblin, Hart	84.9
Ht.	7 Baines, Hutchins, Eldridge, Hutchins	83.8
Ht.	8 Edmonds, Pearce, Maguire, Lancaster	87.0
Ht.	9 Beer, Hart, Jarman, Dallison	86.8
Ht.	10	
Ht.	11 Edmonds, Pearce, Hutchins, Eldridge	89.0
Ht.	12 Blake, Lancaster, Maguire, Barnett	79.0
Ht.	13 Hutchins, Beer, Jarman, Baines	91.2
Ht.	14 Edmonds,	84.0
Ht.	15 Barnett, Hawken,	82.5
Ht.	16 Dallison, Lancaster, Hart,	

Thur 21/5 The format of the meeting followed a more familiar pattern the next Thursday when Ron Johnson won the three major events. Johnno proved supreme in both the Exeter Handicap and the senior scratch race. He also defeated Joe Francis in two straight legs of their match race.

Frank Arthur had been billed to appear but was confined to bed, so instead Francis was brought in as replacement. Perhaps this was fortunate as he was the only rider to challenge Johnson all evening, and finished second in both the major finals. In the Scratch race final Francis suffered engine trouble for three laps, but on the last circuit his machine started to run properly and he made up much ground, but lost narrowly on the run in.

Frank Jarman won the Junior Scratch race. Times were comparatively slow at this meeting as the track was still bedding in after being relaid. Jack Parker, Dicky Case and *Thur 28/5* Ernie Rickman were the main attraction seven days later, but sadly the meeting had to be cancelled because heavy storms had damaged the track to such an extent that racing was impossible. Happily the damage was repaired by Thursday 4 June when an exceptionally good meeting took place. *Thur 4/6*

Half a dozen internationals of outstanding ability contested the Flying Six Match which produced plenty of wheel to wheel racing and fast times. Ted Bravery defeated Bill Clibbett in the opening round and Bluey Wilkinson finished ahead of Ernie Rickman in the second. Tiger Stevenson won the third from Norman Parker. The final produced another win for Bravery, with Wilkinson second.

Heat 1 of the Senior Scratch race produced a spectacular crash. Tiger Stevenson and Bill Clibbett were racing neck and neck in pursuit of Wilkinson when Tiger fell amid a cloud of dust. Clibbett was thrown off balance and flung skywards. After somersaulting through the air he landed head first further down the track. Both riders were shaken and did not ride again, but Clibbett rushed away to ride in the Isle of Man TT races the next day.

The Scratch Race final produced another thriller with Bluey Wilkinson just managing to beat Norman Parker after four tremendous laps.

An International team match between Homelands and the Colonies was the main event on 11 June. This resulted in a 34-17 victory for the Homelands, as Ron Johnson scored more than half the Colonies' points. Scorers were Homelands: Ted Bravery 7 + 1, Joe Francis 7, Nobby Key 7, Buster Buckland 5 + 1, Norman Parker 5 + 1, Harry Shepherd 3 + 2. Colonies: Ron Johnson 9, Bobby Blake 3, Charlie Blacklock 2, Maurie Bradshaw 2, Bert Spencer 1, Dicky Smythe 0. *Thur 11/6*

Bobby Blake won the Exeter Handicap final from Reg Beer and Norman Parker.

Saturday 13 June 1931 saw the opening of Devon's second speedway track forty odd miles down the A38 at Plymouth's Pennycross Stadium. Plymouth was being operated by a completely different company namely Western Speedway, but there were Exeter links. Freddie Hore, the first man to ride the County Ground, was named as Technical Manager and also Clerk of the Course while Bert *Sat 13/6*

Spencer and Noel Johnson were both in the Pennycross team.

The Exeter City team were also present at the opening meeting but were beaten 32-21 in the inter track match. Ted Bravery made his debut for Exeter in this match as did Syd Fuller and Bill Latchem. Buckland started well with two wins but failed to finish in his third outing. The scorers were:

Exeter: Buckland 6, Hawden 5, Beer 4, Fuller 2 + 1, Jarman 2, Bravery 1, Latchem 1. Plymouth: Bert Jones 7 + 1, Maurie Bradshaw 7, Bert Spencer 6 + 2, Peter Slade 5, Spencer Stratton 3 + 1, George Preston 3, Noel Johnson 1 + 1.

Exeter supporters did however have the satisfaction of seeing Reg Robins win the final of the Plymouth Handicap.

Thur 18/6   Billed as the World's Champion, Vic Huxley of Wimbledon, proved his superiority on Thursday 18 June by beating Stamford Bridge's Wal Phillips 2-1 in the match race. Phillips pushed Huxley all the way and won the second leg when the Don punctured a tyre.

The County Ground also saw its first local derby on this occasion when the Exeter City team raced the return leg of their challenge match against the newly opened Plymouth outfit. Exeter gained ample revenge by winning 33-20 and 54-52 on aggregate. Buster Buckland was in superb form winning all three of his heats and recording the fastest time, 77.5 seconds. The scorers were Exeter: Buckland 9, Bravery 7 + 1, Beer 5 + 2, Fuller 5 + 1, Hawken 4 + 2, Jarman 3, Latchem (res) DNR. Plymouth: Noel Johnson 7, Maurie Bradshaw 4 + 1, Peter Slade 4, Bert Spencer 3, Bert Jones 2, Spencer Stratton 0, George Preston (res) DNR.

Reg Beer won the Handicap Final from Ted Bravery. It was announced that the previous evening a meeting had taken place in the grandstand at which a new Supporters Club had been formed. The annual subscription was one shilling (5p) and an attractive club badge was also available at the cost of a further shilling. This badge is now a very rare item and much sought after by collectors.

Thur 25/6   Frank Arthur made a long awaited reappearance on

Thursday 25 June but the Wizard was still recovering from a recent crash and his form was very disappointing. Frank Buckland on the other hand was the outstanding rider of the evening. A bad start in his heat of the handicap eliminated Buster from that event but he made no mistakes in winning both the Flying Four and Scratch Finals as well as setting the fastest flying start time of the meeting, 79.2 seconds.

Buckland defeated Arthur in their heat of the Flying Four match before taking Wimbledon's Ray Tauser in the final, Tauser having earlier beaten Nobby Key of Crystal Palace. Tauser was particularly unlucky to break chains in both finals.

Tom Fardon, Harry 'Shep' Shepherd and Skid Pitcher all rode well but did not figure in the results. Freddie Hawken and Reg Beer had the satisfaction of relegating Frank Arthur into third place in the Handicap Final.

The London team, the Lea Bridge Saints, visited the County Ground on Thursday 2 July for an inter track match and won 25-29. The all round strength of the Saints proved too much for Exeter who's second strings showed a marked inability to score points. Had the Exeter stars received better support there is little doubt that the Londoners would have returned home empty handed. Buckland was in superb form winning all three of his races, while Ted Bravery also did well by winning his first two rides but missed out in his third. However Bravery went on to beat Buckland in the Exeter round of the top scorers match race before defeating Don Durant in the final.

Exeter's 4-2 in heat 2 put them in front until the Lea Bridge pairing of Dook and Lupton notched a 5-1 in the sixth heat. Exeter countered with a 4-2 but after a drawn heat 8 Durant and Alf Foulds wrapped it up for the Londoners with a timely 5-1.

Durant was Lea Bridge's top scorer after being given an extra ride in that last heat. Syd Fuller made his first appearance for Exeter as a reserve.

Exeter's scorers were Buckland 9, Bravery 7, Jarman 3 + 1, Beer 3, Hawken 2, Fuller 1. Lea Bridge (Clapton):

Thur 2/7

Don Durant 9 (4 rides), Roy Dook 7, Stan Lupton 6, Alf Foulds 5 + 1, Reg Stanley 2 + 2.

Buckland also missed out in the handicap final where he could only finish fourth after the other three riders had been given a three second start. Jarman was the winner.

Thur 9/7 Exeter suffered another defeat the following week when they entertained Southampton in the first round of the South Coast Championship. Southampton won by 24-30 and their top scorer was Arnie Hansen with a 9 point maximum. Hansen received good support from Norman Parker and Frank Bond. Beer, Buckland and Hawken fought hard but again lacked support. Exeter could only manage three race wins thanks to this trio.

The first four heats were drawn. Southampton went ahead with a 4-2 in heat 5, but after another drawn heat Hansen and Warren put the Saints further ahead with a 5-1 in heat 7. Although Beer and reserve Ron Coleman hit back for Exeter with their own 5-1 in the next race, Southampton clinched it when Rickman and Parker headed home Bravery and Hawken in the final heat.

Exeter had made several changes to their line-up with Skid Pitcher and George Lovick coming into the team proper and Ron Coleman included at reserve.

Scorers: Exeter: Beer 7, Buckland 5, Hawken 5 + 1, Pitcher 2 + 1, Bravery 2, Coleman 2 + 1, Lovick 1. Southampton: Arnie Hansen 9, Frank Bond 6, Norman Parker 6 + 1, Ernie Rickman 5, Art Warren 2, Vic Collins 1 + 1, Frank Goulden 1, Jimmy Hayes 0.

A new event introduced at this meeting was the One Lap dash. This consisted of four one lap match races. Two between Buckland and Bravery which the Exeter skipper won 2-0, and two between Parker and Hansen in which the former was also twice successful.

Buckland rounded off the evening in fine style by winning the Exeter Handicap final where he came from scratch to beat Syd Fuller, Reg Beer and Skid Pitcher.

Thur 16/7 Owing to the number of league fixtures taking place in London the following week it proved impossible to select a representative side from the Metropolis to meet Devon in a team match. Instead Wimbledon's Ray Tauser and several riders new to the County Ground were booked to appear. A preview of the meeting listed the new faces as Ivor Hill (Wimbledon), Alf Sawford (Crystal Palace), Don Boswell (Stamford Bridge) and new Plymouth signing Paddy Dean.

In the event only Sawford appeared and he was rewarded with second place in the scratch race final, which was won by Frank Buckland. Buckland was programmed to ride a special match race series against Tauser, but the American was replaced by Phil Bishop. Buckland won 2-1.

Sawford also featured with Bravery in a development of the One Lap Dash. This had been extended to become the Two Lap Dash. Bravery won 2-0.

Although no attendance figures had been published so far that year, it was beginning to look as though the promotion was in trouble. Match reports had not appeared in the Express & Echo for several weeks, and another tell tale sign was the announcement that the race night would be switched back to Wednesday for the next meeting.

In fact only one further meeting would take place under *Wed 22/7* the County Speedways banner. That was held on Wednesday 22 July and did attract some big names, in the shape of Lionel Van Praag and George Greenwood, both of Wembley.

Van Praag, who was to make history by becoming the first World Champion in 1936, showed his undoubted class by winning both the Scratch Race final and the 'Big Four' contest. He also set the fastest time of the evening, 79.1, in the first heat of the Big Four.

Buckland and Exeter's other star man, Ted Bravery, both experienced misfortune during the evening. Buckland was matched against Van Praag in the 'Big Four' but crashed. During the rerun Buster suffered a punctured rear tyre. In the final of the scratch event the Exeter skipper was again chasing the Wembley man when he overslid and fell, leaving Van Praag to win from Noel Johnson. Buster remounted and finished third.

Ted Bravery beat George Greenwood in their round of

the 'Big Four', but his magneto packed up in the scratch event. He managed to borrow a machine to ride against Van Praag in the 'Big Four' final but again experienced mechanical difficulties, allowing the Australian to win easily.

The Exeter Handicap was won by Plymouth's George Preston, but his Pennycross team-mate, Paddy Dean, crashed into the safety fence earlier in the evening sustaining facial abrasions. Dean took no further part in the racing.

The Two Lap Dash produced a duel between two long time Exeter favourites, when Noel Johnson beat Bert Spencer in 40.3 seconds.

The Novices scratch race produced the first win for newcomer Bernard Slade who would become a household name after the war. Bernard's winning time was 99.0 seconds.

Despite the change of race night it was noted that there was no perceptible increase in the size of the crowd. Two weeks later it was announced that Exeter Speedway had closed and that the promoting company had gone into liquidation. The Devon and Exeter Gazette reported that their speedway correspondent had received a written communication from Mr Mockford which stated that:

"We have so far this season been running at a considerable loss each week, and of course, we cannot continue on these lines. At the moment we are definitely closed, and have put the company into liquidation. We do not know definitely whether or not anything can be done to enable speedway racing to be carried on in Exeter."

Nothing apparently could be done and so Messrs Mockford and Smith returned to London where they continued to promote at Crystal Palace. It was at the Palace that Mockford introduced the electric starting gate in 1933. This was a joint effort with Harry Shepherd, and successfully overcame speedway's major difficulty, the problem of rolling starts.

In 1934 Mockford and Smith switched their operation to the tiny 262 yard New Cross track where they continued to promote until the Rangers closed down in 1953. During the second world war Fred Mockford won the George Medal for bravery as an ARP warden in the London blitz and was later responsible for such riders as Cyril and Bert Roger and Don Hardy coming to Exeter on loan from New Cross. He died in the early seventies.

CHAPTER SEVEN

1934 EXETER MOTOR CLUB
TRY THEIR HAND

Speedway's initial boom was over. By the end of the twenties more than sixty tracks had opened up, but as the novelty wore off and the bubble burst many including Exeter fell by the wayside.

When Mockford and Smith closed down their County Ground operation in mid season 1931 no other promoter appeared interested in taking over. Obviously if professionals with know-how could not make a success of Exeter nobody else could either. Thus the County Ground track lay unused for two and a half years.

Fri   6/4   However in the spring of 1934 The Exeter Motor Club tested the public's reaction by staging a trial amateur meeting. This took place on Friday 6 April when a crowd of between two and three thousand spectators provided ample proof that interest was still there.

Taking into consideration the unfavourable weather, it was pouring with rain, and the fact that the majority of the riders were local club members, the racing was extremely good, although the track was very bumpy and in need of renovation.

The 500cc class was won by Tom Whitton from Reg Beer and Bernard 'Broncho' Slade, while Ernie Vigers won the 250cc event from Arthur Cox. Whitton was also successful in the 350cc class with Vigers second. A novelty race between Duncan Campbell driving a Morgan three wheeler sports car and Cyril Williams riding a Triumph sidecar outfit was won by the former.

Jack Hawkins, the club secretary was the Clerk of the Course and Mr T. Macleod acted as steward. Although not competing Frank 'Buster' Buckland showed that he was also a talented commentator.

Having adjudged the trial meeting a success the Motor *Fri 20/4* Club embarked on a regular series of fortnightly meetings. For their second meeting the weather was fine and another large crowd turned out to watch the racing. There was plenty of atmosphere, and early arrivals were able to enjoy 'dance music' from the loudspeakers and watch the riders making trial runs. With the announcer requesting patrons to "keep your hands and arms off the fence", racing commenced.

Professional riders were not permitted to compete in the 'Open Race' so that the locals had more of a chance to get among the prizes. The three heats of this event were won by Gordon Taylor, Ernie Vigers and Joe Banks. In the final, Taylor, who was still in his teens, rode a fine race and just managed to pip Bill Martin, who had finished second in one of the heats. Vigers again won the 250cc event.

Plymouth's Bill Clibbett made a single lap record attempt and clocked a time of 19.7 seconds, a speed of nearly 50mph. Clibbett also defeated Ted Bravery 2-0 in their match races, but Bravery rode magnificently from scratch to win the handicap event.

In the local match races Bernard Slade beat Stan Shepherd, Joe Banks headed home Cyril Williams, while Reg Beer defeated Gordon Taylor.

By Friday 4 May the track was in perfect condition and *Fri 4/5* the third meeting was an outstanding success, with a crowd of almost 4,000 present.

There was little to choose between the local riders in the Open Race. Freddie Hawken, Tom Whitton and Dingo Davey were the three heat winners with Hawken narrowly winning the final from Whitton. Ernie Vigers notched his third consecutive 250 win, this time from Don Blackmore.

Topping the bill were the 'Four Star' match races. In the

first Ted Bravery disposed of Bill Stanley 2-1 while Bill Clibbett followed this up with a 2-0 victory over Bert Spencer. Despite his defeat the 'Baby Cyclone' rode with all the spectacular dash that had made him such a favourite at the County Ground in 1929.

Clibbett took advantage of his inside gate to head Bravery in the final, but after spraying his Plymouth team mate with cinders for two laps he finished alone, as Bravery pulled out with engine trouble.

Fri 18/5 The next meeting, which took place a fortnight later on 18 May, was equally successful although the ACU had put a bar on registered professional riders competing on tracks less than one mile in circumference unless they were in the National Speedway League. Despite the absence of the professionals it was reported that this was the best programme yet put on by the Exeter Motor Club. Close finishes were the order of the day along with customary thrills and spills. However an ominous cloud was cast over the occasion by the much reduced size of the crowd, which was way down on previous meetings.

Freddie Hawken had things very much his own way with seven wins from nine starts. Freddie also returned the fastest time of the night during his match race with Tom Whitton, which he won in 88.0 seconds. In this race Hawken roared away from the outside gate, passed Whitton on the first bend and won comfortably by 30 yards.

The other match race saw Max Sweeney defeat Francis Drake in a time of 97.0 seconds.

The 'Open Race' saw heat wins by Hawken, Bill Willmott and Broncho Slade. Hawken rode another clever race in the final where his superior cornering again kept Whitton at bay.

Whitton took his revenge in the handicap final when, despite some determined attempts, Hawken was unable to find a way through. Stan Shepherd was third.

Fri 1/6 The rapid decline of public interest brought the 1934 season to a premature end on Friday 1 June, when a team match between Devon and Cornwall attracted less than 800 people.

The match was raced over just three heats. Freddie Hawken won heat one from Cornwall's Bill Jones while Stan Shepherd was third to give Exeter a 4-2 advantage. Francis Drake, a good Devon name if ever there was, was unlucky in the next race. First his machine began to play up and then he lost his goggles. Although Whitton hung on to second place behind Willmott, Cornwall were able to level the scores. In the third and final heat Bert Jones' bike failed to start and then Whitton crashed on the second bend of the first lap leaving Hawken to head home Willmott giving Devon a 9-8 victory.

The best race of the evening was seen in the final of the limited handicap event. Reg Beer, with a two second start, won from Bert Jones on scratch. Jones made the fastest time of the meeting when he won the Scratch Race in 89.4 seconds.

The meeting's only casualty was Bernard Slade who twisted his knee badly during his match race with Jones and was forced to withdraw.

Sadly it was announced during the evening that due to lack of support no further meetings would be held for the time being. Obviously the Exeter public, who had grown used to seeing the best riders in action at the Country Ground were not so keen on supporting the amateurs and had lost interest. Bernard Slade endorsed this theory at the time of Exeter Speedway's Golden Jubilee in 1979. He told me;

"The fans were used to seeing the riders broadsiding around the bends, but when the likes of Ted Bravery and Bill Clibbett were prevented from racing, that extra excitement was missing and the public simply lost interest."

The Exeter Motor Club's foray into speedway promotion was short lived and the County Ground would have to wait for another thirteen years before the roar of the bikes was heard there again.

SPEEDWAY RACING COMES BACK TO EXETER THANKS TO —

R. P. JONES — FRANK (BUSTER) BUCKLAND — BERNARD (BRONCO) SLADE.

THE SHERIFF OF EXETER (F. P. COTTEY ESQ) MEETS THE "STAR" RIDERS —

FRED TUCK — ROY CLARKE (Belle Vue, Manchester).

THAT'S CHARLIE SPINKS

AUSTRALIA.

STIL 1945.

CHAPTER EIGHT

1945 THE POST WAR REVIVAL

Speedway was not seen in Exeter again during the thirties, although some of the local riders went on to further their careers at other tracks. Frank Buckland rode for Crystal Palace before retiring while Broncho Slade also had rides at the Palace before joining Hackney Wick. However the coming of the second world war was to put a sudden stop to speedway throughout Britain, and in fact one of the first casualties was to be the 1939 World Final at Wembley.

Happily with the ending of the war in Europe in May 1945 there came a rekindling of interest in speedway at Exeter. A group of local enthusiasts, among them Frank Buckland, Bernard 'Broncho' Slade and Bill Eastmond, felt that the forthcoming Victory in Europe Day celebrations would be an excellent reason for putting on a meeting. They formed an organisation called the Exeter Speedway Motor Club and soon found that they faced monumental problems in getting their idea off the ground. Only Belle Vue, Manchester had succeeded in staging regular meetings throughout the war years, and many of the riders were still in the forces.

Slade had been involved in the aircraft industry during the war and had managed to ride in the occasional charity meeting at Rye House towards the latter part of hostilities so knew which riders were available with necessary machinery. Amazingly Broncho signed up no less than twenty riders who were all keen to take part.

The next problem was finding a suitable venue. The County Ground had been commandeered for military purposes early on in the war and was for some time home for thousands of American GIs prior to D-Day; among them world heavyweight boxing champion Joe Louis. By the spring of 1945 the Yanks had gone and while greyhound racing had returned, the stadium was not yet available for speedway racing. With no other stadia in the area it was decided to mark out a 360 yard grass track on Bill Eastmond's land at Exwick fields directly behind the Thatched House Inn, with financial support coming from several local businessmen.

Mon 21/5   The European Victory Meeting took place on Whit Monday, 21 May. Unfortunately the weather was extremely wet. So much so that several lorry loads of sawdust had to be sent for and laid on the track. Despite the rain a crowd of 8,000 turned up to watch the racing. Broncho had come up trumps with the riders and the twenty strong field included such stars as Wing Commander Bruce Semmens, who had spent the war piloting Sunderland flying boats, Fred Tuck, Ron Clarke, the 1944 British Open Champion, and Old Etonian Mike Erskine.

The meeting took the form of an individual event and was won by Fred Tuck, who with Ron Clarke had driven down after racing at Belle Vue the previous Saturday evening. No easy journey at that time.

The non-experts final was won by local rider, Clifford Plain, who had been in second place and had taken full advantage of the situation when the leader, his cousin Herbie Plain, had mistaken the last lap flag for the finish and slowed up. Other locals taking part were Reg Robins and of course Broncho Slade.

The meeting was a tremendous success and the profits, a sum of £200 were donated to the Sheriff of Exeter's Appeal for the St John Ambulance. The Sheriff was none other than Mr F. P. Cottey, one of the original directors of Southern Speedways.

Such was the success of the Victory Meeting that the organisers, encouraged by 'hundreds of requests for the real thing' wasted little time in looking for a suitable site where they could construct a proper track. Obviously it would not be long before the County Ground was once again available, and indeed plans were already being made to turn it into a first class stadium as part of Exeter's post war rebuilding. Meanwhile a temporary location for the speedway was found at Alphington on a piece of ground beside what is now Alphin Brook Lane. This site was later developed as Baker's Yard, the well known surplus warehouse.

Lack of the right materials forced track builder Bill Eastmond to use his initiative and improvise. A 250 yard circuit was cut out, the turf and top soil of which was removed and used to build the safety fence. Cinders formed the track surface and washing facilities for the riders was provided by the Alphin Brook which flowed through the little stadium. The whole place was built in little more than a fortnight and the opening meeting took place on Thursday 5th July.

Thur 5/7

In the editorial of the first programme Buckland explained the difficulties that had been overcome to get the Alphington project off the ground.

'With little or no material (wood or steel safety fence being unobtainable), we have managed to build, what we hope will turn out to be, one of the most spectacular tracks in the country.

It is not our intention to make this our permanent home, mainly because the ground will not be sufficiently large to hold the crowds of tomorrow, and in any case we understand the ground is earmarked for industrial purposes. But after an exhaustive search in and around the city, this site was the most suitable of those not requisitioned by the government.'

Not surprisingly there were few facilities for the public, other than chairs for those prepared to pay the top admission price of 4/6d (22p) for the privilege of sitting down. A few days before the first meeting the War Agricultural Committee threatened to serve a 'Plough up Order' on the organisers. Although this was averted the promoters were forbidden to do any more work on the ground, as Britain was still effectively at war with Japan and war restrictions were still in force.

Another good line-up was assembled headed this time by that great favourite from Exeter's pre-war days Ron Johnson. Tuck, Clarke and Erskine were also present, and were joined by Vic Warlock and Fred Brown from Bristol, Alex Grey (Harringay), Reg Lambourne from Worcester, who was later to become a well known race horse trainer, Art George (Bruton) and Roy Zeak (Cardiff) plus of course locals Broncho Slade and Reg Robins.

The track was extremely dry and the racing produced clouds of dust. There were no hosepipes or any equipment with which to water the track, and a frantic call to the National Fire Service for a pump to spray water from the brook went unheeded.

Just as on the original opening night in 1929, Ron Johnson was the star of the evening. The little New Cross Ranger won all his heats and the final, with the exception of heat 4, when he reared at the start and fell. He also set the fastest time of the meeting which naturally was also the new track record, 63.2 seconds. By now all races were clutch starts, although Alphington did not boast the luxury of an electric starting gate.

Circumstances dictated that the meeting started promptly at 7.00pm even though double British Summer Time ruled out the necessity for floodlights which naturally were also unavailable. The early start was to ensure that the racing was over by 8.30, the time that the last 'A' bus left for the city centre. Wartime petrol rationing was still very much in force so fans had the choice of relying on public transport of walking home.

Thur 12/7   The following week's meeting, a 'Pairs Championship', went even better. Records are a shade unclear as to which pairing actually won, but the track record was broken no less than five times, ending up at 61.0 to the credit of Belle Vue's great leg trailer Oliver Hart. Hart set his record time in the very last race of the night, the 'Fliers Final'.

This race developed into a neck and neck tussle between Ron Johnson, Bill Kitchen and Hart, with the Belle Vue rider snatching victory by half a length from Kitchen. Johnson ran into machine troubles during the meeting and rode Reg Robins bike for much of the time. Canadian Eric Chitty also made his first Exeter appearance.

The meeting was marred when Broncho Slade took a heavy tumble in his fourth ride and was taken to hospital with concussion and a broken collarbone thus bringing his season to a premature end. Broncho had been somewhat unhappy when he found himself listed in the programme as BRONCHO SLADE — HACKNEY WICK & "WILD WEST KENN !!". He accused Buckland of sending him up but in later years realised that it was only an example of Buckland's showmanship.

Three new faces appeared at this meeting Ron Howes, Ken Harvey and Frank Lawrence, all from Wimbledon. Ron Howes was partnered with Oliver Hart. During 1988, the Diamond Jubilee of British Speedway, Ron was the President of the Veteran Speedway Riders Association. At the VSRA's celebration at the site of the original High Beech track Ron recalled how he had travelled down to Exeter from London with Lawrence to race at Alphington.

"I remember that it was a very long journey in those days." He told me. "We borrowed an old trailer to take the bikes down on, but it was not until we started on our way home again that Frank realised that the trailer had no lights. We came to some road works and Frank shoved me out of the car and told me to nick a couple of oil lamps which we hung on the back." Ron did not recall much about the racing but the trailer lights obviously stuck in his memory.

As already mentioned details of these Alphington meetings have been hard to find. There were no specialist speedway magazines at that time and the contemporary newspapers were very thin and full of such historic events as the post war General Election and the dropping of the atomic bombs on Japan, therefore the Express & Echo appears to have had no space to report on the challenge match between England and Dominions on Thursday 19 July. It *Thur 19/7* took place, and I have a partly filled in programme to vouch for it, while a later programme refers to Oliver Hart reducing the track record to 58.2 in this match.

Thur 26/7   Seven days later 'Devon' were due to take on the 'Rest'. Alas heavy rain during the day caused the ACU Steward, Mr George Allen of Southampton, to abandon the match at 5.40pm following a track inspection.

Thur 2/8   The weather was kinder the next week when a second England v Dominions match was staged. Promoter Buster Buckland pulled off something of a coup when he persuaded former Wembley star Colin Watson to lead England. Watson had retired in 1936 after breaking his leg, but had now ridden three times in London since the war. The nine year break did not stop the County Ground track record holder from leading the Lions to victory and personally notching up 12 points, as England won 39-32. The other England scorers were Hart 9, Kitchen 8, and Tuck 7, while for the Dominions Eric Chitty, Malcolm Craven and Wilf Plant scored 6 points each. This meeting was particularly well supported with between four and five thousand fans present, many of them climbing the surrounding trees to get a better view.

Thur 9/8   The next attraction was a North v South team match which featured all the regular riders and ended in a 39-39 draw.

Thur 16/8   The season came to an end on 16 August with the staging of the official ACU Southern Championship. Between seven and eight thousand people packed into the little makeshift stadium, and were rewarded with the best racing seen at the track. The racing was extremely close and several times the riders were three abreast on the track. Not surprisingly there were also several crashes. Colin Watson was carried off with concussion, and in heat 14 Ron Clarke and Wally Lloyd collided while battling for the lead. Oliver Hart was following close behind and tried to avoid them, which allowed Bill Kitchen to nip through for an unexpected win.

In the final, Kitchen made the start with Eric Chitty and Ron Johnson in hot pursuit. For three laps nothing separated them, but the last time around Chitty overslid and carried Johnson out to the fence, thus allowing Kitchen to get away and win the Championship. It was a magnificent finish to what had been a tremendously successful revival of Exeter Speedway, and a fitting finale for the temporary stadium which would never again be used for public racing.